Photographic *Memories*

INTERFACES: STUDIES IN VISUAL CULTURE

Editors Mark J. Williams and Adrian W. B. Randolph, Dartmouth College

This series, sponsored by Dartmouth College Press, develops and promotes the study of visual culture from a variety of critical and methodological perspectives. Its impetus derives from the increasing importance of visual signs in everyday life, and from the rapid expansion of what are termed "new media." The broad cultural and social dynamics attendant to these developments present new challenges and opportunities across and within the disciplines. These have resulted in a trans-disciplinary fascination with all things visual, from "high" to "low," and from esoteric to popular. This series brings together approaches to visual culture—broadly conceived—that assess these dynamics critically and that break new ground in understanding their effects and implications.

For a complete list of books in the series, visit www.upne.com

PHOTOGRAPHIC MEMORIES

Private Pictures, Public Images, and American History

ROB KROES

Dartmouth College Press *Hanover, New Hampshire*

Published by University Press of New England Hanover and London

Dartmouth College Press

Published by University Press of New England,

One Court Street, Lebanon, NH 03766

www.upne.com

© 2007 by Rob Kroes

Printed in the United States of America

5   4   3   2   1

Library of Congress Cataloging-in-Publication Data

Kroes, Rob.
Photographic memories : private pictures, public images, and American
history / Rob Kroes.
    p.   cm.—(Interfaces: studies in visual culture)
Includes bibliographical references and index.
ISBN-13: 978–1–58465–596–1 (cloth : alk. paper)
ISBN-10: 1–58465–596–8 (cloth : alk. paper)
ISBN-13: 978–1–58465–593–0 (pbk. : alk. paper)
ISBN-10: 1–58465–593–3 (pbk. : alk. paper)
    1. Photography—United States—History.   2. Documentary photography—
United States—History.   I. Title.
TR23.K76 2007
779—dc22   2006030878

For Marianne,

My new haven

Contents

Foreword

Donald E. Pease

Rob Kroes's *Photographic Memories,* as the distinction between "private pictures" and "public images" in its subtitle implies, is concerned with the interplay between highly personal and profoundly public memories. Kroes wrote the book to come to terms with the fear that following the death of his first wife, Sioe Kie, his second marriage would result in "new emotions and a new involvement that would, like a sedimentary layer in geology, cover and then smother memories of Sioe Kie." Trying to heal the wound that was left by his wife's death led Kroes to invent far-reaching strategies of mourning. The book correlates Kroes's effort to work through this traumatic transition in his personal life with Europe's collective effort to achieve the transition from the cold war epoch that Kroes shared with Sioe Kie to the time of a European Union.

Photographic Memories emerged out of Kroes's sense that photographs supply a storehouse of affective images through which individuals and cultures archivize their memories. Building on this insight, Kroes aspires to undertake an individual as well as a collective work of mourning. In accomplishing this correlation of the personal with the collective work of mourning, Kroes brings his nuanced account of the role photographs played in enabling him to come to terms with this devastating personal loss together with his sense of the public usage to which these photographic memories could be put in effecting the transformation of cold war history. In the course of the book Kroes establishes profound interconnections between the photographs in his private family album and the "photographs of history" that have become part of the collective memory of the peoples on both sides of the Atlantic.

Kroes organizes his book by establishing and explaining disparate connections between the highly personal and the collective. More specifically, Kroes produces what might be described as an afterlife for his personal family album in the epic encounters that he adduces between the history of photography and the photographs of history. The book moves from photographic memories of the American Civil War and the cold war as these archives inform Kroes's desire for the transformation of Europe into a European Union.

Kroes elaborates on the relationship between his personal mourning and Europe's collective acts of mourning by exploring the role that iconic photographs in particular play in forming a larger public's collective sense of history. According to Kroes, iconic photographs resemble cultural myths and the legends with which they are associated in that all three of these artifacts exceed the intentional control of the cultures out of which they emanated. Kroes describes the prototypical iconic photograph as a memento mori: it freezes a moment in time that is past forever following its exposure; such as it was it will never be again. The "savage silence" of iconic photographs freezes transient motion into what Kroes calls a "lasting stillness without words."

A nostalgic medium, a photograph looks at the present in the light of an awareness of things passing forever. Iconic photographs possess what might be called the power of epic concentration, condensing the tragedy of history into a single arresting image. When iconic photographs freeze history into memory, they make us feel as if they have done the work of memory for us. They come to us like documents from the other side, last wills and testaments that are drawn up in the service of personal and collective memory. But iconic images are unlike documentary film footage in that they don't lose the sense of the decisive moment by turning it into just one more passing moment. Upon entering into the mass circulation of images, iconic photographs are endowed with the power to affect history rather than merely produce reflections of it.

The book's second chapter, "Photography and Immigration," supplies a key to understanding the book's deeper symbolic action as an act of filiopietism whereby Kroes would refind his place within the symbolic order by restoring the relationship between living and dead Europeans. In this chapter, Kroes's research achieves an exhilaration that derives from his bringing people, like W. G. Sebald's great-uncle Ambros Adelwarth, and their forgotten times back to life. In Sebald's *The Emigrants*, nameless faces are restored to their place in history through stories told by distant offspring. These American photographs serve the psychological purpose of shoring up the hopes of immigrants.

Overall *Photographic Memories* reflects the spiritual journey of Sebald's extended family from the time of his ancestors' emigration to America to his own recent return to Europe. This cyclical journey led Kroes to a profoundly expanded sense of the duties and obligations pertaining to his sense of filiopietism. Kroes elaborates on this ethical dimension of his project in his discussion of Steichen's photo installation "The Family of Man." In widening the camera angle from the private family of Rob Kroes to *The Family of Man,* Kroes enlarges the symbolic embrace of his act of filiopietism so as to draw his readership into a quasi-familial circle, whose reach would aspire to include the entire planet. Whereas the photographs in personal family photo albums serve to document life's irreversible moments (birth, baptisms, bar mitzvahs, death), Kroes's retrospective on the significance that he discerned in Steichen's photo installation transforms "The Family of Man" into a sign of promise for all the inhabitants of the planet.

Whereas some commentators criticized "The Family of Man" for its collapsing of the political into the familial, Kroes finds the quasi-familial gaze valuable for its conjoining of established European and American ways of looking at the world so as to redescribe that gaze as a universalizing picture. Upon acknowledging that the space of identification of Steichen's exhibition may indeed be the restricted space occupied by the western European and the European American's bourgeois nuclear family, Kroes refuses to endorse the accusation that this perspective is constitutive of an imperial optic. Instead, he discerns in this imaginary space a humanistic familial ideal and an aspiration toward universal communication that resonated with Europeans' desire to work through the traumatic afterlife of World War II.

Kroes continues Steichen's effort at reuniting Europe in the wake of the cold war by recollecting in his penultimate chapter the uncanny realism in Sebald's *The Emigrants* or his later novel *Austerlitz.* "Imaginary Americas in Europe's Public Space" examines the role that Europe's image of the Americas can play in the EU's construction of the image of a larger Europe. Kroes wants his meditations on American photographs to contribute to efforts to turn Europe into a *lieu de mémoire,* the sort of space that emerged from Sebald's journey across space and time. He wants to reanimate these memories of the dead so that the extensive family album of Europeans can be reunited through these memento mori of the dead Europe. "We need to construct Europe as its own underworld with ghosts wandering about demanding to be heard," Kroes writes apropos of this transformation. "We need photographs documenting a Europe long since vanished."

In the final chapter, "Shock and Awe in New York City: 9/11 or 9-1-1? The Construction of Terrorism through Photographs," Kroes records his uncanny experience of finding himself reflected in the faces of those who were about to die and who silently called out "Forget me not!" But this traumatic experience threatens to shatter rather than complete the profound work of individual and collective mourning that preceded it.

Acknowledgments

Given this book's daring scope, taking the reader from my own autobiographical perspective to areas where my own memories interact with memories I hope to share with others, I felt in need of the sympathetic and supportive reading of friends and colleagues. I circulated the manuscript among them and benefited greatly from their comments. Their views gave me the necessary support to continue with the project as published here. I wish to thank them and mention their names: Volker Berghahn, Marc Chénetier, Kate Delaney, Maurice Gonnaud, Marianne Hirsch, Mick Gidley, Monique van Hoogstraten, Heinz Ickstadt, Marianne Mooijweer, Mary Nolan, Donald Pease Jr., Jay Prosser, Marja Roholl, Robert and Kiki Rydell, Rob Silberman, Alan Trachtenberg, Marilyn Young, and my two sons, Remco and Quinten. A grant from the University of Amsterdam allowed me to spend the first half of 2003 at New York University's International Center for Advanced Studies, then involved in a three-year project on the Cold War. Its focus, during the time I was in the inspiring midst of it, was on the culture of the Cold War. My chapters on Cold War photography could not have been written without the inspiration of my colleagues at the Center.

Photographic Memories

INTRODUCTION

BOOK TITLES should be self-explanatory. Yet mine needs further explanation. I chose it not for its precision, but for its ambivalence. In just two words it is suggestive of more than a single theme for this book. Its ambivalence straddles two themes that for many years have kept interacting in my mind and have directed my reflections in the following set of essays. The two themes are photography and memory. My interest is in their interplay.

Memories are stores of sensory perceptions, of sounds, of sights, of smells and touches. Memories and photographs only resemble each other, or rather, overlap, to the extent that they are visual representations of actual occurrences, things that took place before our eyes or before a camera lens. They take the form either of inner images or of photographic pictures. The first we may only hope to share with others using language and its narrative conventions as a medium of communication; the second, owing to its form of objective visual documents, we can share with others, without any requirement of mediation, by simply showing them. We all remember those first days back at work after the holiday season, when most of the first morning is whiled away looking at colleagues' vacation snapshots. Yet what makes these mornings memorable is the enthused running commentary accompanying the individual shots. Clearly the latter trigger a repertoire of memories, turning the taker of snapshots into a teller of stories. The individual photographs become embedded in a context of tales, and we remember them in their narrative setting. Photographs, at that point, have become a medium in their own right connecting us to other people's inner images. More than that, their photographs have become part of our own inner store of images. We remember such photographs along with the storyteller and the stories told. We even remember ourselves sitting and listening, stirring our morning coffee.

Photographs are often referred to as mnemonic devices, as memory aids, as tools that help us to remember what we wish to remember. The rationale of family albums is precisely that: the documentation of family life as parents wish to remember it. Revisiting old photographs, going over the family album, is intended to trigger the reservoir of inner images, of memories. Pointing to pictures, people will exclaim: Ah yes, do you remember what happened here? And stories will begin to flow. Yet such revisits can also be painfully disturbing, offering a remembrance of things past while making us realize the passage of time, as an unstoppable process of aging, of losing loved ones, of losing touch with people scattered across the globe. Looking at photographs is always a confrontation with loss, if not death.

Among writers about photography Roland Barthes is arguably the one who has most perceptively explored this changing meaning and message of photographs over time. There is the unforgettable description of a photograph of his mother as a young girl, standing next to her little brother in the winter garden of their family home.[1] This photo of his mother as a child is read by her son after her death, a son who in a sense had become her "mother." While caring for her, a frail old woman in her last illness, Barthes felt as if he "engendered my mother." Now that she is dead, he can only look forward toward his own death. He can read that death in her picture. Her first picture, read by her son, is also her and his last, the picture of the mother/child. Barthes's reading of his mother's photograph vividly conjures it up before our eyes. So vividly indeed that it comes almost as a shock to realize that the photograph is actually not in the book. It has come to us as a prose picture that, more than evoking the photograph itself, draws us into Barthes's reading of it, into his intense effort to catch its meaning and render it in verbal language. If Barthes can recognize his mother's essential being in the winter-garden picture of her, it is possible only through the description and narrative in which he articulates his response to her image. In his book, his mother's picture exists only in the words he uses to describe it and his reaction to it. Language in this case serves as the sole medium to render the intricate mental processes, going back and forth between photographs as visual documents, memories as inner images, and the quest for meaning, for interpretation. Words can do this because of a power of language that is literally "metaphorical," a power of "translation," whereby words transcend themselves as feeble descriptive tools to trigger our imagination, helping us "to see."

Language, then, is the only tool we have to allow us to communicate with others about our individual experiences of the visual, or for that matter the auditive. I have always been an avid reader of texts about music, whether they analyze compositions or evaluate musical performances in words that an audience has in common. Similarly, I have always been intrigued by the many ways that humans have developed to write about their visual experiences, be they photographs or memories, inner images. Writing the essays in this book, this is what I saw as my central challenge: to try my hand at various ways of writing about the visual. The essays are in that sense what French author Raymond Queneau called one of his books: *Exercices de style.*[2] Photographs always triggered my exercises, photographs as they related to my life as an American Studies specialist. They ranged from the highly private sort of pictures—such as photographs that now form my family album or the uses that immigrants made of photographs in their continuing relationships with family and friends in their countries of origin—to public images, such as press photographs, that have become part of the collective memory of people on both sides of the Atlantic. More often than not, even in this latter case, there was a connection to my own private store of remembered pictures. Thus, for instance, the chapter on "The Family of Man"—a massively successful exhibition of photographs—is more than an exploration of the ebb and flow in the critical reception of the show. It also felt, while I wrote the chapter, like a revisit of images that I had long stored in my memory. At the time the show came to Amsterdam in the Netherlands, I was too young to go there myself, but I remember the enthusiastic response of my older sister. She brought home the catalog and I eagerly went through it. Many of the pictures burned themselves into my memory, as if on an etcher's plate, and came back as remembered images when I began my exercise in writing about the show in its Cold War context.

If one of the themes in this book is the relation between memory and photography, as they connect to American history, one of the recurring ironies is that photographs as public images have become remembered pictures themselves. Our contemporary sense of history is replete with photographic memories. When I ask a group of students what comes to their minds when the topic is the Vietnam War, their association is with visual images, remembered photographs, or for that matter Vietnam film images. As I argue in the chapter on the American Civil War, this sea change in the collective memory of epochal events occurred when photography first showed the photographic face of war to the general public. Ever since, photography has preserved its power to condense historical drama into single, iconic pictures. In a separate chapter, an intermezzo forming a bridge between the sections on private pictures and public images, I explore this power of iconic photographs in forming a larger public's collective sense of history. Yet, as Alan Trachtenberg in his seminal *Reading American Photographs* reminds us,[3] photographs often derive their meaning from the order of an album or a series, accompanied by interpretative text. This particular reading of the power of photographs is more akin to my exploration of collections of photographs, as in "The Family of Man," or Robert Frank's *The Americans*.[4]

Another lifelong interest of mine has been the way in which America's visual representation of itself in Europe's public space has affected the sense of collective identity of Europeans as "Europeans." As the map of Europe kept changing from Cold War days to the latest eastward expansion of the European Union, America has been a continuing presence as a cultural "Other," providing Europeans with a counterpoint in their collective search of their emerging identity. Much of that presence has been visual, presenting views of the good life in a tempting construction of Americanness. As I argue in a separate chapter, much of the creative response to this presence in Europe may well be read as visual messages of Europeans exploring novel collective identities, rather than as simple signs of cultural resistance to "America."

Although my memories of visual images are a personal point of reference in much of the writing in this book, as an interpreting subject I fade in and out of focus. I am most clearly a presence in the opening and closing chapters of the book, giving personal testimony to an almost existential urge to use photographs to help me find my bearings in a bewildering world. Those two chapters serve as personal bookends to a collection where I try to keep my private motives more at bay and maintain a more Olympian distance to the subject of my fascination.

Widening its angle from the private to the public, this book might be said to take the reader from the family of Rob Kroes to the Family of Man. As exercises in remembrance these writings are, despite the obvious differences in angle and scale, attempts at exploring the suturing power of photography, its power to heal the wounds inflicted by history or the mere passage of time. Photography may help people to reach closure in their attempts to cope with tragedy and trauma. As the reader will see, my return to my family album as well as the writing that it inspired followed "a death in the family," the sudden loss of my wife. Trying to read the changed meaning of my family album and the memories it unleashed allowed me to reach closure through my writing. For a more public "album," the "Family of Man" exhibition, suture and healing were central to its mission to transcend the Cold War divisions of the world and the threat of nuclear annihilation that hung over it. The exhibition is now on permanent display in its final resting place in Luxembourg, the birthplace of its curator and designer, Edward Steichen. The exhibition's continuing appeal has invited new readings of its implied messages.[5] The Cold War may be behind us, but the World War II Holocaust has come back to haunt our collective conscience. As we shall see in a later chapter, it is possible to make a powerful case for the "Family of Man" addressing the trauma of the Nazi genocide. The show omitted direct visual evidence of genocide, yet a close reading of the pictures on display may help us detect narrative ploys that evoke the enormity of what happened while suggesting connections between a prewar past and the postwar birth of the state of Israel. This may have worked as one of the exhibition's subtexts, but only if we assume that the mid-1950s public of the exhibition shared a collective memory of the concentration camp photographs that were in mass circulation in the immediate postwar years.

The connection between photographic memories and trauma is much more direct in the case of the terrorist attack of September 11, 2001, the topic of this book's last chapter. The event was instantly seized by the news media. Television footage and newspaper photographs allowed the whole world to be a witness. Yet, locally, there was a different need for visual documentation, for photographs that local residents had collectively produced and went on to display in an impromptu show of about five thousand pictures, taken by three thousand photographers, in an empty shop fifteen blocks away from the disaster. Initially in the nature of a therapeutic self-help venture for those affected, the project expanded into a photographic documentation exercise intended both as an archive and as an alternative media publicity outlet. It showed what local people had seen and what they wished to remember in a display of visual control taken back from the media. A selection of photographs from the show went on tour to a number of cities in the United States and Europe, at locations including the MoMA in New York (February–May 2002). The instigator of this project, Michael Shulan, in summarizing its particular characteristics, describes it as not so much a conventional art exhibition as an improvised memorial for the dead and an exercise in documenting the monstrous, with the fundamental principle that it is open to anybody and everybody. As Shulan writes in the introduction to the exhibition's catalog: "in order to come to grips with all this imagery which was haunting us, it was essential, we thought, to reclaim it from the media and stare at it without flinching."[6] Surprisingly, then, the catalog ends with the ultimate symbolic gesture of suturing: the concluding pages show us a view of the Manhattan skyline intact once more. As if time were cyclical, a return to the past may suggest a view of the future. Only so, in cyclical time, may one hope to reach closure.

 PRIVATE PICTURES

ONE ◉ ARRESTING MOMENTS

Revisiting My Photo Biography

MY EXPLORATIONS OF AMERICA, as a traveler and an academic, have coincided with my life as a married man. They also ran parallel to my adoption of photography as a way to store and preserve moments and views that struck me as memorable. I had dabbled in photography before, but as a man newly married, traveling to the United States for the first time with my wife and a three-months-old baby boy, there was a new sense of urgency to my use of the camera. Over the years a veritable memory bank has built up, recording my family life in the many different places, in Europe and the United States, where we traveled or lived for longer periods of time. I had always been aware of my inclination to use my eyes as if they were a camera lens, taking mental pictures. To use a common metaphor, I had a photographic memory for people and places. The camera would, I felt, help me keep doing what I had always done. Photographs would double as external copies of my inner mental prints, facilitating access to my store of memories.

Then, after thirty years of a happy marriage, my wife suddenly died. I took my last mental pictures. I can still see myself before my mind's eye kneeling down beside her prostrate, lifeless body, crying out her name in panic, hoping beyond hope that she had only fainted. In the weeks following her death my inner album was in disarray. To my utter dismay I found I was no longer able to conjure up her face, either as a still photograph or in motion, so richly expressive of her inner emotions. What had happened to my mind, to my memory? Had she died there as well?

Shortly after, trying to handle my feelings of loss, I went over the many photographs in the family album. I chose several fairly recent portrait photographs of my wife to enlarge and put up in my living room. I had a different fear then, that the photographs, rather than trigger my mental pictures, would forever blot them out and take their place as vicarious memories. While frantically trying to remember her, wasn't I in fact busy forgetting her? As it turned out, my fears were unfounded. After a while, the lock on my inner store of pictures gave way and my wife appeared in my dreams, in motion, talking to me, walking by my side. In my waking hours her face appeared before my eyes, uncalled but always welcome. I could separate photographs of her, which I could call up at will, from her pictures in my mind taken with my eyes.

This brief, anguished episode made me more consciously aware of the intricate workings of memory, and of the intricate relations between mental pictures and those produced by mechanical devices. The idea began to form in my mind that, starting from my own recent experiences, I should more generally explore the relation between memory, history, and photography. Ever since the invention of photography and motion pictures, both have provided the human reflection on memory with central metaphors, helping us to understand the way people form their individual and collective stores of memories. Some memories, like those of President Kennedy's assassination, are called "flashbulb memories";[1] others are called "filmic." But both media have done more than simply provide metaphors. As recording mechanisms they have actively intervened in the way people "see" their world and make sense of it. Sometimes photographs have the greater power of the two, condensing the enormity of an event into one iconic picture; sometimes films do this, transporting us to places and times otherwise inaccessible, showing us events as they happen. In each case, though, what we remember are transmitted images, mediated events. Throughout this book, I will gradually open my lens, starting from the highly personal and private, which got my reflections going in the first place. Then, in following chapters, I shall explore pictures and images as they affect larger publics. But throughout those chapters my concern is with the central triad consisting of mental pictures as an inner memory bank, of photographs, and of films.

What is the difference between photography and film? From one angle the difference is a matter of quantity. Film in this view is merely a series of still photographs, chronologically arranged. If we wish, we can look at a film reel frame by frame, picture by picture. A stranger to our technological culture would have no clue as to the mysterious power lurking in the minute differences between one frame and the next. Today even children know the mystery and can produce jerky motion from a series of simple drawings rapidly flipped through. So, from another angle, the difference between photography and film is qualitative. The difference is a matter of turning a series of still photographs into what is so appositely called a motion picture. It is an ingenious invention that tricks the human eye into perceiving motion where all that is presented to it is a series of stills. The motion produced by motion pictures is an illusion, based on the inertia of human perception. As an illusion it finds its analogue in reality, not in the medium that carries it. Film does not capture the continuity of movement the way that a musical recording reflects in perfect analogy the continuity of sound.

Movement, in the sense of visual continuity, has always puzzled the analytic mind. From antiquity to the age of Bacon and Newton the paradox appeared unavoidable that the smallest conceptual unit of motion was its negation, that the dynamics of motion could be conceived in no other way than as a series of moments of *stasis*. The very logic of the Newtonian differential calculus is based on this paradox, reducing the continuity of a curve to a number of tangential points along it approaching infinity. Film is nothing more than the application of this logic to a machine, the "movie" camera. Increase the number of shots and the illusion of continuous motion will result.

There are many ironies in the history of this invention. At an early stage, in the famous series of still photographs of motion by Eadweard Muybridge, motion was purposely reduced to moments of stasis precisely to show what escaped the human eye because of its inertia. Thus Muybridge could show that a galloping horse at certain points had all four feet off the ground. He consciously used the power of still photography to explore the unconscious optics of human perception, the *Optisch-Unbewusste*, as Walter Benjamin would later call it. What Muybridge did was daringly illustrate the power and mystery of still photography, its power to capture precisely those transitional moments in the continuity of motion that no human eye has the power to perceive.[2] The inventors of film would build on his findings but would take them in the opposite direction, using still photographs to represent motion. Ever since, both forms of mechanical reproduction have gone their own independent ways, developing diverging canons as to the proper use of the two new media.

Yet there are moments in the history of film where film pays tribute to the medium that spawned it, still photography. They are moments where, in an act of self-conscious awareness of the logic of the motion picture, a filmmaker freezes one of the frames and, much like Muybridge, reduces motion to a still photograph. All of a sudden narrative flow and visual continuity come to a full stop, in a moment that is arresting, literally and metaphorically. The power of still photography is called upon to produce an image of epic concentration. All of a sudden the projecting beam seems to turn back to us like a laser burning its image into our minds. It produces what we might call an arresting moment. It was famously used by François Truffaut in *Les 400 coups* (The 400 Blows) and other French *Nouvelle vague* directors and carried to the logical extreme of a film consisting entirely of stills by Chris Marker in his *La jetée* (The Jetty).[3] American film directors influenced by the French New Wave, such as Arthur Penn, used the device to equal effect.

A similar awareness of the power of still pictures to present arresting moments may come from comparing film footage and still photographs, when they both document momentous historical events. As examples, let us take two iconic photographs that probably linger in the mind of the reader: "Viet Cong Executed," a 1968 photograph by Eddie Adams, and "Terror of War," a 1972 photograph of napalmed children by Nick Ut. I will talk at more length about those photographs later, but here the point I wish to make relates to the force of iconic photographs compared with documentary film footage. As it happened, neither Adams nor Ut were the only witnesses around. There were other photographers at work by their side, as well as cameramen shooting film. The two moments captured by Adams and Ut, as it turns out, were also recorded on film. Bringing the two media together, as I did on several occasions teaching a class on photography, makes the different impact of both media dramatically clear. In the case of the Adams picture, as the photographer put it referring to Vietnam's national police chief, who was the willing executioner: "When he fired, I fired." Adams produced "a picture that shook the world," as Associated Press general manager Wes Gallagher called it. Despite the impression of the sole and alert witness that the photograph itself appears to convey, Adams was not alone. But he might as well have been. Compared with film footage, where the execution is over before the viewer is aware of what truly happened, Adams's picture catches the unconscious optics of the moment, capturing the chilling composure of the executioner and the contorted face of the victim just prior to or at the exact moment when his skull is hit by the bullet. Similarly with the Ut photograph. There is color film footage showing the children—the grass by the roadside is green alright—sort of fluttering by, arms up in the air, crying. The camera follows them, but there is nothing like the impact of Ut freezing the moment in his unforgettable photograph. The still photographs seem to tell a story more fully than film reproducing movement. They have what we may call a power of epic concentration, condensing the tragedy of history into a single arresting image. In such photographs all the various rays of light relayed to us through modern mass media of communication appear as if condensed into a single burning laser beam.

In that sense still photographs are but a technical means to satisfy the ingrained human habit to take mental pictures, to look at certain moments with the urgent sense that here is what must be remembered. Only since the advent of photography have we used metaphors derived from the new medium to describe what human beings have always been doing. I do it when I speak of "taking mental pictures." Yet what the metaphor describes, I remember doing at many points in my own life. It is a double remembering. I remember myself at moments when I wished to remember (which probably testifies to the success of the endeavor). Once, as an eleven-year-old, at the end of what stands out in my memory as a glowing summer vacation with my parents in the Austrian mountains—our first such trip abroad in the early days of European economic recovery after World War II—I remember turning around on my seat in the bus, looking at the mountains as they receded in the distance, and saying to myself: "Look! Remember this!" I have been back in the area many times since and can almost remember the spot where I took "my mental picture." There is much willfulness involved in this. Taking the mental snapshot is an act of will, and so is the later return to these inner pictures. At other times, though, the inner album opens un-summoned, springing surprises, either joyful or painful, on the unsus-pecting mind. Later in my life I returned to the Boston area as a visit-ing lecturer, having spent a semester there five years before with my wife. I was alone the second time around. My wife had died a year after the first visit. It was not a happy return. I could not turn a corner or walk a street without images leaping at me. There were hair triggers all over the place opening my inner album of pictures without notice. I began to realize that the place itself was inscribed with my memories, while at the same time holding the key to my inner album. I felt a strange urge to go back to places where we had been together, although I sometimes had to force myself to do so, feeling the strength drain from my knees. There were pictures all over the place, waiting to be visited by the single sur-vivor of the happy couple that had lived there together. They were like so many fragments that—only through sheer magic—I might hope to re-member, to paste together again into the fullness of a past where death was not yet the looming presence it turned out to be. I remember listening to many musical renditions of the old Orpheus story, feeling like him in my imaginary descent into an underworld stored with hair-trigger memories.

They were all memories that brought my wife back to life. I had not seen her die, although I was present in the house, so I had no memory of her face turning into a still picture, a death mask. I found her on the floor of the hallway, prostrate. When I turned her over, her face was frozen into an expression of wonderment, eyebrows slightly raised in surprise, her mouth set as if asking a last question. The thought never came to me to take her photograph then. It would have felt like a dese-cration. I looked at her and took my last mental picture.

Every photograph can be seen—and has been seen by other writers about photography—as a memento mori. It freezes a moment in time that is past forever following its exposure. Such as it was it will never be again. Photography is therefore a nostalgic medium. It looks at the present in the light of an awareness of things passing forever. It is a medium of memory, an instrument that parallels the power of the human eye and mind to see and remember. It is an instrument, though, that also helps the human mind to remember life and to beat death at its own game. According to its intrinsic logic, photography does not produce death masks, with life drained from them. It may of course produce pictures of dead bodies, or of dead faces, yet the fact that photography as such freezes time and brings life to a full stop makes the matter of life and death irrelevant. The lens simply records what is within its purview.

I have witnessed only two dear ones die, my mother first, then my father a little over one year later. They had been divorced for well over a decade. Theirs had not been a happy marriage. When my mother lay dying, I was by her side. It seemed that all she had become were two pensive, observant eyes, introspective more than interactive. I have no idea what went through her mind. She spoke no more. It must have been a last picture show, replaying her life and her memories of it. Then the light in her eyes went out. She kept breathing heavily for a long time. I was by her side, whispering little stories into her ear, memories we shared, hoping that somewhere inside her head she would hear and understand, and relax. Then the breathing too stopped. I looked at her face. A gentle whirlwind seemed to sweep across it, causing her face to ripple and wrinkle, as in a fast-motion replay of the process of aging. It was over in a matter of seconds. Her jaw sagged, her skin tightened around her eyes, mouth and nose. Her face turned into a death mask. I realized that what always escapes our perception, but is always there as an unconscious optics—the process of aging—I had seen before my eyes *as process,* as motion, racing toward its ordained dénouement in death. Of course I had been aware of my mother's aging, particularly in the rapid decline of her last years, but only by comparing moments of stasis, comparing recollections with current observations. Strangely, I never felt much need to go back to actual photographs, either before or after her death. There never was much of a family album in the first place. Mental pictures served my purposes of gauging the flow of time and the changes it brought perfectly well.

My father's death affected me differently, for a number of reasons. When my wife and I reached the hospital, he was already in coma. Hours before, his kidneys had stopped functioning and he had been given a shot of morphine. He was beyond human communication. As it was, there were too many people around, talking to each other, missing the moment that is still etched in my memory when his lips gave out a final, little puff of breath. It looked as if he blew out his own candle.

Photography played a different role in the case of my own married life. It would be different again after I lost my wife. Throughout my married life the camera was like a fifth member of the family. I was the one to wield it most often, but regularly my wife insisted on taking photographs as well, with me in them. I remember a recurring, though inarticulate, resistance at having my picture taken. The family album we thus "coproduced" consists mainly of slides chronologically stored and covering the entire span of our life together, but also of prints, either in color or black-and-white, taken in the early years when our two sons were small. The slides we watched every now and then, when newly framed slides, as yet unseen, were added to the store. These sessions always ended, mostly at my wife's request, with a return to the past. Let's see some babies, she would say. After her death a novel sense of urgency drove me to go over the thousands of pictures. Many assumed a new poignancy for me, at times hard to bear. Two relatively recent portraits of my wife in particular leapt out from the screen, as if she had sprung back to life. In one her face fills the entire frame. She almost seems to break out of it, with the welcoming, joyful smile that greeted visitors to the house. The other shows her, half in profile, in a more pensive mode, with assessing, monitoring eyes as if she was taking the measure of something outside the frame. I had the two slides printed and enlarged, as a memento for my sons and myself. I put mine up in the living room in central position. Frantically trying to suture the wound that my wife's death had caused, inventing strategies to negotiate the transition in my life, I was engaging in a photographic practice that is as old as the invention of photography. From that moment on, photographs of the living have always been used as mementos of the dead. "Forget me not" is what such photographs then come to say.[4]

In much recent work on the subject, family photographs appear mostly as a distorted representation of family history. The look at family life that they provide is partial, to say the least. They are also partisan, skewed toward a remembrance of happy moments, of togetherness. In their typical form they are mostly staged, with family members posing in obedient subservience to a set of unspoken choreographies, in shared rituals of self-representation. One can almost hear them say "cheese" in humorous unison. In a highly perceptive study of the implied rules of choreography, Erving Goffman highlighted the unconscious body language of the actors in family photography, the way they tuck their heads in gestures of deferent submission, stand or sit, group themselves together, look up or down, have arms around shoulders, or hold hands, in a complex theatrical staging of family relations, gender relations, relations between generations and siblings, between man and wife. Even in the more recent age of an increased self-conscious awareness of such strategies of self-presentation, of increased informality in family relations, as well as of increased sophistication in the uses of photography for family purposes, these tacit conventions have survived to a remarkable degree. I for one am often surprised when I take my camera in hand and look through the lens at friends and their children, over at my house or on a joined outing. The moment they see me do this, as if acting on cue, they stop whatever they are doing, look into the camera, produce smiles, and regroup into standard formations. Not always, though, not everywhere. It would be interesting to explore whether there are national or generational differences in family photography, or whether it is solely a matter of individual taste and preference.

Whatever the answer, in my own case taking pictures of my family always formed a larger project. It was quasi-journalistic in its attempt at recording family situations as if there were only my eyes taking mental pictures. More often than not that was the cue on which I acted, saying to myself: "This you must remember." I ran to get my camera, hoping the scene would still be there for me to record. When I was too late, I thought of Christopher Isherwood's famous opening words: "I am a camera," wishing it were true. On other occasions it worked; I was back in time and shot many pictures that appear to be unobserved. Of course, one never knows. Children being natural actors, mine may well have internalized my expectations and may have—endearingly, I must admit—staged the informality that I wanted my pictures to have.

What else was the point of my project? Here is a big irony. My photography project ran parallel to my view of my married life as a project. Or better: as a dream. My dream was to have a happy family, to bring happiness to it, to feel happy in it. As I now see it, my urge to document all this in photographs was to be able to show them to my parents. I certainly felt the presence of their eyes looking over my shoulder as I took my pictures. It was a belated effort to bring them comfort at a time when I no longer lived in their house. It continued a role I remember myself assuming from the time I became aware of their pained relationship.

By and large the album of photographs of my married life resembles so many others in the image it conveys of a happy family. But it is an image that I consistently worked in my married life to make a true reflection of a real state of affairs. Of course here as elsewhere it takes two to tango. My project for my marriage could easily have failed, as it takes two people who each have the talent, or the will, in the daily round of married life to keep their eyes fixed on their transcendent sense of themselves as a couple. My wife and I were able to sustain that sense. We shared the romantic sense of the family as—to quote Christopher Lasch's book title—a haven in a heartless world. We were equally romantic in sharing dreams of exploring the world together, venturing out as a family of four (we had two sons in the first four years of our marriage), sharing experiences, and building up a store of shared memories. As it happened, America played a continuing role in those explorations. I'll come to that in a moment. First let me introduce my wife.

She had been born of Chinese parents, in the city of Medan on Sumatra, in what was then the Dutch East Indies. She was the last child in an already large family. The father worked as a self-employed silversmith. As my wife told it, she was given away upon her birth to the family doctor, a member of the white colonial elite, in an act not uncommon in South China or the Chinese diaspora in Southeast Asia. Giving a child away formed part of an established custom to weave quasi-familial links outside biological family groups, spreading the risk and creating larger networks of interdependence and exchange. The doctor and his wife, Gregor and An Krause, had no children. My wife was the second Chinese daughter they adopted. From two different families, the girls grew up feeling and bonding like sisters. The foster parents insisted on having the girls stay in touch with their biological parents. But it wasn't long, as my wife remembered it, before she looked at her Chinese parents and siblings with the estranged sense that they looked so Chinese. Apparently, she had already begun to internalize the physiognomy of her foster parents as her standard for the perception of somatic difference. Or more correctly perhaps, she became aware of the cultural mold that sets the range of facial expressions and body language. As I recollect it, her facial expressions never struck me as exotic, or Oriental, but rather as Dutch. I have always thought of her, from the time we first met, as a Dutch person in a Chinese body. Yet, growing up, she must always have been keenly aware, in the Indies and then, after the war, in the Netherlands, of the disparity between how she felt and the way she looked in the eyes of others. The manner she had developed for negotiating the disparity was through a self-deprecating irony, conveying a sense that there was more there as a person than the eye beheld, a greater cultural commonality with Dutch people than her Chinese looks might at first suggest. Her very name had a ring of endearment to Dutch ears. It was given to her by her foster father, based on two Chinese characters meaning "embroidered twig." In its Dutch transliteration (Sioe Kie) it sounded like "See you key."

We met as students in Amsterdam when we were both teaching assistants in the Sociology Department. I was in my midtwenties. Everything I know about her past is based on what she told me about it or on the rare family snapshots that she had in her possession. She felt no great urge to do so, to go back with me over her peregrinations across the globe. But even so I gained a sense of the remarkable itinerary she had behind her when we first met. Sumatra to her basked in the golden glow of childhood memories, of life in Medan, of time spent on Lake Toba, where her parents had a summer house to get away from the oppressive summers in town. On at least one occasion she spent a furlough with her foster parents in Europe. There are a few photographs of the girls in the snow in Switzerland, eyes wide open in surprise at what happened to them. While the parents traveled in Europe, the girls were left in the care of Catholic nuns, and baptized in the process. It was more a protective measure than an act of faith on the part of the parents. This way they knew the girls would be in good hands, as my wife remembered it in an ironic tone. Upon their return to the Indies, it wasn't long before war broke out. Soon the family found itself interned in Japanese concentration camps, the two Chinese girls with their white foster mother in a camp on Sumatra, the father in a camp on Java. The utter irony of it! Two Chinese girls treated as members of the ruling Dutch colonial elite, yet in fact so westernized in their comportment and facial expression that later on people from mainland China, trying to account for the incongruence they noticed, took my wife to be Japanese.

Unlike her sister in later life, my wife was never troubled by what became known as the so-called concentration camp syndrome, a violent return of repressed memories haunting the survivors and upsetting their mental equilibrium. She did carry memories with her throughout her life of the stench and dirt surrounding the sanitary pits in the camp, of the slimy excrement left by the many who suffered from dysentery and could no longer control their bowel movements. In my wife's case memories like these may have led to a measure of obsession with the control of bodily functions. Yet it never affected her mental health and stability or her capacity for ironic self-reflection. Memories that would come back to haunt others she managed to keep on a short leash.

All four members of the family survived the war and were reunited following the Japanese surrender. The father, an erudite and polyglot introvert, had managed to continue to lead a life of the mind while interned. He had been able to take several editions of his beloved Dante with him and had filled the margins scribbling Chinese poetry from memory. The books are still in my possession, and I look at them as a remarkable testimony to the powers of the human mind under duress. I never knew him. He had died before my wife and I met. Born in the 1880s in what was then East Prussia, part of the German Reich, he moved after his medical studies there to the Dutch East Indies, pursuing his dreams of adventure and exploration. In the employ of the Dutch colonial army, while still a German national, he spent time on the island of Bali. It was still relatively untouched by Western civilization, although it had its resident colony of artists. Like Gauguin venturing out in quest of the paradisiacal exoticism of Tahiti, Gregor Krause must have felt similarly driven. His tool to record what his eyes beheld was not the painter's brush, though. It was the camera. He combined an anthropologist's inquisitiveness and the aesthetic eye of the photographer to produce an album of Bali photographs, published in Germany in the 1920s, that would establish his international reputation. The photographs document religious rituals, ceremonies, dances, but they also show more intimate scenes of Balinese people, in stylized poses that convey Krause's Orientalizing romanticism.[5] Later he would move to the island of Borneo and work as a physician for a Dutch oil company. He would produce another set of photographs there, portraits of the apes and monkeys of Borneo, almost humanizing these close cousins of mankind. This set too would be published in Germany, like the Bali photographs with an introductory text by Krause. Sumatra was Krause's next station. He had become a naturalized Dutch citizen by then, and began work as a self-employed family physician in Medan. Only then, no longer in their prime, did he and his wife adopt the two Chinese girls. As my wife on occasion summarized it in jest: "First they took monkeys into their house, then us."

Following reunion, the family moved to Australia with the idea of settling there for good. In fact they did not stay for much more than a year. Although the episode was remembered glowingly by my wife, leaving her with a lifelong nostalgia for Australia, I sometimes wonder whether Australia's "whites only" immigration priorities did not make the Krauses reconsider their decision. They may have wished to spare their children a future of racial denigration and injury. It may also have been due to the restlessness both Krauses shared. Whatever the case, they decided to "repatriate"—a buzzword at a time when so many among the colonial elite in the Dutch East Indies foresaw the end of Dutch rule. It is an inept word for two Chinese girls from half a world away moving with their foster parents to the Netherlands.

The family odyssey first led to The Hague, the traditional crossroads of Dutch and Dutch-colonial society. Krause was a practicing physician there for several years. A highly private man, he spent much time with his books, immersing himself in Catholic philosophy of a neo-Thomist bent, or with a small circle of artist friends. One of them did a drawing of my wife, then a thirteen-year-old girl. It still hangs in my house. With her long, black hair in two braids, she very much looks like the *jeune fille rangée,* the charming, well-groomed daughter of a middle-class bourgeois family. Yet her eyes directly confronting the artist's intent gaze show a subdued anger, a resistance to bowing to the will and whim of other people. There is a sense of this adolescent asserting her individuality, already being her own independent woman. It is the woman I recognize in the second of the portraits I put up in mourning, the one with the pensive, monitoring eyes. The other portrait reflects her other side, open, warm, welcoming, radiating a readiness to please others. That is what kept her by her mother's side after Gregor Krause had died. The family had moved once again, following Krause's retirement, to an old Saxonian-style farm in the eastern part of the Netherlands. For him it would be the last station of his worldly itinerary. By then the older daughter had already left the house, marrying a man considered below the family's social rank. Her quest for independence caused tension in the family. Following the father's death the mother cut off all remaining ties. With my wife, the balance went the other way. Loyalty and filial bonds kept her by her mother's side, despite the whimsicality and restlessness of her mother's character. The compromise location they found was a small village, close enough to Amsterdam for the daughter to pursue her academic study and for the mother to lead the life of a "snowbird," flying off to her second house on the Spanish coast whenever the spirit and the weather moved her. Yet the place was far enough removed to make for a life in relative isolation, for a setting that would keep the daughter from any rival bonding.

This might have worked, were it not for the fact that Sioe Kie was hired as a teaching assistant. This would take her out to Amsterdam much more often than just her final work on her master's thesis. That is when she appeared in my life. We shared an office, and worked on joint assignments. We became good friends, and I was invited to her place "to mow the lawn," as she put it. She may in her own unassuming, ironic way have been making advances. Yet it was a while before the decisive moment of epiphany when I saw her in an entirely different light. We happened to have season tickets to twentieth-century-music concerts in the Amsterdam Concertgebouw, and we had gone there independently before the time we first met. One Sunday I was early and sat by myself at a table in the lounge. I felt a little sad and lonely, in postadolescent weltschmerz. Suddenly (I had not seen her come up to me), there was her melodious voice over my head, simply greeting me, saying "Hello, Rob." It sounded like a little, tinkling bell; it felt like the touch of a magic wand. I heard music before the concert had begun. We were a couple from that moment on, and got married within a year.

I told this story to the gathering of friends and relatives, her coffin by my side, on the day of her funeral. Reminiscing, going over memories as they had leapt at me during the preceding days following her death, I told the audience that just two months before we had celebrated our thirtieth anniversary. Then going back in time I told the story of the Concertgebouw, and I could hardly get myself to repeat the two simple words of greeting she had spoken. Suddenly I choked and felt a sobbing rise up in me. Pausing for a moment, getting myself together again, I then said, "Hello, Rob," words that I knew could only be followed by those final two words: "Good-bye, Sioe Kie."

When she died, all that was left of a happy marriage were my memories, the pictures in my head, and the family album of photographs.

They appeared to me in an entirely different light then. The book had been closed. They were no longer the open-ended collection of stills that together formed the film reel of our life, open to the future. No further stills could be added, trying to catch the flow and motion of married life. The film itself had come to its end. The only arresting moment I decided to add was a photograph of the imprint of a pigeon's body, wings spread, on the picture window of our living room. The bird had bumped into it the morning of the day my wife died, as a harbinger of what was to come, a messenger of death. The ghostly image, clear to the eye only when the sun was at the right angle, formed the closing shot, the final arresting moment, of the film.

My life has changed once again, and so has my view of my family album. If there is a "before and after" division in my sense of my family photographs, critically set apart by Sioe Kie's death, a third episode has now begun. Since March 2002 I have been a married man again. I had known my new wife for many years. She had been my student, my research assistant, and then a graduate student whose dissertation work I supervised. She had been to my house; she knew Sioe Kie and had attended her funeral. We had not been in touch since, until we resumed contact in early 2000. I had been vaguely aware—one did not much touch on such extramural matters—that she felt stuck in an unhappy marriage. She was going to ask for a divorce. It did not take long for a second epiphany to happen to me in my life. We saw each other with different eyes; we had fallen in love. I took my camera out again, this time to make portraits of her. My great fear then was that new emotions and a new involvement would, like a sedimentary layer in geology, cover and then smother my memories of Sioe Kie.

Fortunately we can talk about this at length. Marianne, my new wife, is actually eager for me to tell her about my life with Sioe Kie. She wishes to go back with me into my past and get a better sense of who I am now. She engaged with me in finding a transition, rather than insisting on a clean break with the past. She insisted on keeping Sioe Kie's photographs up in the living room. Only I added photographs of her, of equal size, standing side by side with Sioe Kie's pictures. I could look at them and weave my two lives together. Photographs provided me with a means to put my two loves, and lives, on a par.

One powerful tool to help Marianne form a picture of my past and fill in a blank is my store of photographs. Amazing things happen to me when we have these sessions. Spurred on by her eagerness to see pictures of my past, I no longer see them as a film that will never be set in motion again. Old enthusiasms rise again, as I am transported back to the moments I took these pictures, often remembering why I took them, what I felt taking them. Stories resurface which I tell Marianne, flipping from one picture to the next. It feels like being airborne, swirling like a swift bird over my past life, from times when my sons were babies to their more recent past as adults, from Sioe Kie with a young mother's pride nursing an infant to her later features of a woman enjoying social events with colleagues at her workplace, or with friends in the village, a woman with her own purpose in life, radiant with a quiet, inner strength. I become aware of strange, unsettling paradoxes. The older the photographs, the younger the faces they show. There is so much future in the early pictures, so much past in the more recent ones. I also realize there is an inner tape rolling inside my head, synchronized with the "moving" pictures on the screen. The tape brings back the viewers I had in mind when taking my pictures, my sense of whose eyes were looking over my shoulders, my sense of which people I wished would share my gaze. It comes back to me now that much of my early family photographs were taken with my parents in mind as an imagined audience. Of course at the same time my picture taking was a work of memory, feverishly catching on film what my mind's eye saw and wished to preserve as memories to be shared with my family. The latter impulse is probably the one stable drive recognizable throughout the entire collection. Yet here again I have to face up to the fact that time has affected the meaning I wished my pictures to carry. Viewers I had in mind, watching my pictures, listening to my running commentary to provide them with context and focus, have died, one after the other. New viewers have appeared—Marianne in particular—whom I never had in mind while taking the pictures. I have to readdress the messages in them, rephrase their meaning.

I had dabbled in photography ever since my high school years, but never with anything like the sense of a continuing project until I got married. I was almost twenty-seven then. That was truly the moment where my life as an adult started. I had just graduated in the social sciences. I had won a fellowship that would take us to the United States for well over a year. And I had a new camera, a single-eye reflex.

Given my wife's itinerant life and my own eagerness to explore the world with her, we did not wish to settle down. Although we had a house in the Netherlands, we thought of home as any place where we would be together. Within a year we had our first child. Three months later we crossed the Atlantic. The grant I had received from the Commonwealth Fund in New York, known as a Harkness Fellowship, was regal. I could go to a university of my own choosing. We were expected to travel widely and explore the country. A car was waiting when we arrived. I remember feeling relatively neutral about going to the United States. At a conscious level I had not been particularly drawn to the country. I had in fact taken Soviet Studies as an elective rather than American Studies. All I remember in terms of eager anticipation was the prospect of going to the University of Chicago, the place as I then saw it where a truly American sociology had developed. It had been a sociology whose central fascinations were with the cosmopolitanism of urban life, as it unfolded right outside the university's ivied walls, and with what would be called—in language fashionable now—the construction of identities and social meaning through human interaction. As it turned out, my reading of Chicago School sociology was as good a preparation for life in America as any American Studies course I might have taken.

But nothing, not film, not books, prepares greenhorn visitors for the raw clash with reality. Arriving in New York on a hot July day, we huddled together in a small midtown hotel room, overwhelmed by street noise, police sirens, by high-rise buildings dwarfing us. Like scared snails we felt like pulling in our eyes and withdrawing within our shells. The baby, overdressed as if we had expected winter, lay steaming in his stroller. That first shock, of course, does not last long. We began to venture out and to take in the new world around us.

Our horizon widened slowly. After a few days we moved into rented rooms in the east seventies, at walking distance from Central Park. The house was owned by Charles Kikuchi, a Japanese-American who had studied sociology at the University of Chicago and whose diary, which had just come out, of life as a young man in one of the "relocation centers" during World War II my wife and I would soon read. That too was a way of widening our horizons, gaining a sense of the immense variety of life experiences in America. It also allowed us, my wife in particular, to see connections between lives lived half a world apart, between her life as an internee in a Japanese concentration camp and his life as a Japanese-American in an American concentration camp. The ironies involved in their experiences may well have produced the broader sense of irony that Kikuchi and my wife shared.

Those summer weeks in New York were a time of feverish exploration. I documented daily life in the apartment, strolls in the park, trying to catch the glow of quiet contentment and happiness of my wife. I often ventured out on my own, driven by a sense of urgency and excitement to catch street life through my lens, to photograph buildings or their reflections in other buildings, the old as it struggled to hold its own against the relentless onslaught of the new, building sites, billboards, the city by day and the city by night, as it turned into a nightscape. I was accosted by hookers but did not dare take their photographs; I ventured out in Harlem, down from Morningside Heights, and, playing the uninitiated foreigner, did dare ask people: Could I take their picture? I ventured upon a young black man doing a crayon portrait of his girlfriend. We started talking, and he offered to do my portrait. It was done quickly, showing a definite likeness although with slightly African features. He held it up and I photographed him.

My relentless drive then to photograph everything, from my small family circle to the larger setting of Manhattan, I remember as having been inspired by two motives. One had to do with a sense, which my wife and I shared, that these were the first moments of our new life together. A number of things coincided in this shared sense of novelty. As a couple we had set out on a voyage of married life, eager to explore what that life would bring us, what it would mean for the two of us. We lived in eager anticipation of what was in store for us. But this sense of having taken a daring, existential leap together found its perfect reflection in our physical voyage, leaving the narrow confines of life in the Netherlands and seeing the world open up like a wide-screen spectacle. America, more than any European location, is the place to offer this sensation. It is one of the crucial ingredients of America as an imagined place in people's minds all over the world. In my case, it must have lain dormant in my mind and was triggered into a rush of adrenaline only upon setting foot on American soil.

If this fevered sense of urgency was one driving motive, as well as one motif in my early photographs, the other motive once again was to make my parents part of our joint excitement. In fact I sent my rolls of film to the Kodak laboratory in the Netherlands for development, and gave my Dutch address for delivery of the slides. That address is where my parents stayed during our absence, as house sitters. My parents eagerly looked forward to receiving my photographs and the letters that my wife and I wrote to give them a sense of context and help them interpret what the photographs showed them. Our foreign exploits gave them a common focus.

The year 1968, in which my wife, baby boy, and I went to the United States, was a time of great political excitement. As it happened, I missed out on most of the action. Columbia University had already had its student occupation when we got to New York. I walked across the campus and had friends who had been active in the protest movement point out buildings that to me were only names from newspaper reports in the Netherlands. Following our time in New York we lived near Boston for a few weeks when the Democratic Convention took place in Chicago, with its pitched battles between police and demonstrators in front of the convention hotel. Like so many others we watched the events on television. Again, once we had reached Chicago to spend the academic year there, I could only stroll around after the event and project my mental images on places and settings that had recently been the scene of such violent clashes. Later that year, though, student protest would catch up with me. The University of Chicago would have its own student occupation. I entered the occupied buildings with my camera, told wary student guards that I was on their side, sharing their cause as a graduate student in Amsterdam. They took my word for it and allowed me to take photographs. I wasn't lying much, although I overstated my activism. By inclination I am more of an observer from the sideline, but in fact my interest in the protest movement turned into a dissertation on the subject a few years later.

Looking back at the store of pictures taken during that first total immersion into American life, I see that they achieved my primary goal (satisfied my primary motivation). These photos document, first and foremost, our private experience of exploring America's space, of ever widening our horizons, moving free and unrestrained as a self-contained family unit of three. We looked inward, watching our son grow in a process of two-parent bonding; we looked outward, taking in the huge canvas of America's cultural regions, its natural scenery. There was a constant sense of exhilaration, which comes back now when I revisit my pictures. Often in the pictures the inward and outward looking converge, showing mother and son, or father and son, as they travel through American space.

Friendships are another theme in these photographs. Friends we made, from our time in New York on through the year, several of whom would be lifelong friends, appear in the pictures and would reappear in later years, in pictures taken in Europe when they came over to see us or in America on one or another of our later visits. As in our case, they had children whom the pictures show at various stages of their lives. Like us our friends grew older, visibly aging as time moved on. As in my case, death came to visit them. The wife of a dear friend, whom we first met in Chicago, radiant with life, reappears as a mother of one, then of two children. They are all in the photographs, at various stages of their family life. Then, years later, in the late 1980s, her face appears when she was in the midst of a long-drawn struggle with cancer. Its expression is one of fatigue, mixed with a desperate will to live and stay with her children. These were then in their midteens. It was all to no avail. In the end she gave up and had her life brought to an end, in the circle of her family. The husband came over to see us in the Netherlands, seeking our support in his time of mourning. Not long after, he would fly over to comfort me.

When we returned to the Netherlands, our lives had changed. The country and its culture felt even narrower than before, its concerns of no great moment when looked at from an outsider's perspective. That is precisely what I, more than my wife, had gained, for she already had a personal history of peregrination and cultural crossings. For all practical purposes we now shared a sense of distance from the country we lived in. Yet at the same time, widened as our spiritual orbit may have been, the Netherlands still felt like our central point of gravitation, a place of emotional mooring. We did not wish to leave it for good, but only to keep our options open to resume our orbital movement. As it happened, upon my return to the University of Amsterdam to resume teaching at the Sociology Department, a position opened up in the American Studies program. The man in charge of the program, Professor A. N. J. den Hollander, also chaired the undergraduate program in sociology. Sensing my enthusiasm about my time in America, he suggested moving sideways from sociology to American Studies. I jumped at his suggestion and have never regretted my decision since. I became his successor as chair of American Studies in the mid-1980s. I followed in his footsteps in more ways than one. I shared his intellectual curiosity in the ways that Europeans had imaged and imagined "America." Like him I became president of the European Association for American Studies, moving in a larger European world of colleagues in the field, enjoying the diversity in disciplinary perspectives that they brought to the study of America. Ironically, for an American Studies person, one of the joys was the taste of what it ideally might mean to lead the life of a European. Here was a circle of friends and colleagues, from all European countries, including what was still Eastern Europe at the time of the Cold War, using English as the language we all shared. Over the years I taught and lectured at many different places in Europe. I used English more and more as my writing language as well, with a view to intellectual communication on a scale far larger than the Netherlands. My books were increasingly published in the United States rather than in the Netherlands.

I may have become Europeanized over the years; I have also become Americanized. I move effortlessly among Americans, aware of their social codes and conventions, and I share their sense of scale. Their country has become part of my inner map of a world I feel at home in. Small wonder, then, that I have been back many times. But always, if possible, with my home team, my family. Not of course for the flying visits to a conference, but for visits lasting months. We have lived in many different places; we kept traveling widely. My two sons spent a year going to school when we lived near Washington, D.C., just across the district line in Maryland. They were in their early and middle teens at the time. Always my camera was there as a witness. The initial excitement might have abated somewhat. America had to a certain extent become known territory, *terra cognita*. Yet superimposing itself on it, the ever-changing face of my family kept adding novelty and intrigue. How would the exposure of my two sons to America affect their inner horizons, their sense of themselves? How would their mixed descent, being half Chinese, half Dutch, be perceived by American classmates in school?

Race or skin color had never played a role in our family history, as I remember it. Certainly there was ethnocentricity, if not racism, in the Netherlands at the time when residents of the former Dutch East Indies, many of them of mixed Eurasian descent, "repatriated." Yet my sister had married a man of Eurasian descent precisely at that time, in 1958. Never had my parents objected to their engagement on such ethnocentric grounds. Nor did they in my case. Used as I was to my parents critically commenting on my choice of Jeanne Moreau look-alikes, they opened their hearts to Sioe Kie from the moment I introduced her to them. Her being Chinese was never even mentioned. They must instantly have recognized the Dutch person inside her—more than that, the endearing human being she was. Looking back, this is remarkable testimony to the humane liberalism of my parents. As for my two sons, I remember only one moment in the Netherlands that may have bruised them, particularly my older son, Remco, who is the more Mediterranean looking of the two. Visiting friends in the provincial outback of the country, we took a Sunday afternoon stroll through their village. At one point a swarm of little urchins surged from a garden, shouting: Negroes, Negroes!!!

Nothing like that ever happened during our many visits to the United States. If anything, our sons' disregard of outside appearance, of somatic signs of "race," made for an openness to people regardless of color. I have photographs of black girlfriends coming to the house in Silver Spring, Maryland, or, for that matter, later on to our house in the Netherlands. I remember a story my younger son, the more light skinned and blond-looking of the two, told us. When he was found out overhearing a conversation among black female classmates of his, discussing their views of white boys, one of them turned to him and said, including him in their circle: "You're not white, Quinten, and you should know it." In an ironic tone, which he had in common with his mother, he shared this story with us. We had a chuckle. As my photographs show it, we had friends of different color over at the house. My sons—most likely, wittingly—straddled borderlines that may have felt more forbidding to their American friends.

There is one episode where my photographs lose their familial focus, in terms of either subject matter or intended audience, and enter the realm of, as Marianne Hirsch would have it, the quasi-familial. The episode is among the few in which I ventured out on my own for a longer period of time. My wife had not been able to negotiate and organize a leave from her job for that long. I spent the winter of 1988 in Bozeman, Montana, to do research on a Dutch-American farming community west of Bozeman. My family and I had been to the area before and more or less stumbled upon the place. An exit sign for Amsterdam and Belgrade—an unusual combination for touring Europeans—seemed like an invitation we could not turn down. We drove around the rolling hills of the western part of the Gallatin Valley, with farms spread out across them, and reached a residential node, Church Hill. Amsterdam itself, it turned out, was not more than a crossroads, a blacktop road crossing a railroad feeder line, long since in disuse, with the empty shell of a grain silo as a nearby marker of past business. There were Dutch names on the mailboxes, little windmills on many of the front lawns. A plan hatched in my mind to come back and do a community study. I took back with me a volume produced by the Gallatin Valley Historical Society, with the names, photographs, and brief genealogies of many of the people in the area. I went to the local cemetery and photographed some of the headstones on graves of early settlers.

Once back in the Netherlands, I was able to trace many of the families to their places of origin. Work in the provincial archives helped me to flesh out the scant information that I had brought home with me. Also I decided to visit the places where many of them had come from, and take photographs there. I also took more pictures at burial places where forebears of Gallatin Valley settlers had been laid to rest. I had in mind using such visual material for a public presentation following my return to the Dutch-American community. In my research in various Dutch archives I had also come upon collections of letters sent home by the early settlers. One such collection allowed me to follow one family in particular, from settlement in the 1890s until well into the 1920s. I came to share their daily concerns as if the letters were addressed to me. It felt as if I had become a vicarious family member. One moment was particularly gripping. The letters whose ink was fading let me in on the news that the wife was expecting a baby. Then there is a gap in the correspondence. When it resumes a baby boy's name is mentioned as well as the name of a woman, a relative from the Netherlands, who must have come over recently. As I could make out from later letters, the mother had died when she gave birth to the baby.

When I returned to the Gallatin Valley, a historian friend who teaches at Montana State University in Bozeman had arranged for my public presentation at the gym of the Christian School in Church Hill. Preparing for the event in my room on the university campus, I went over my notes and arranged my slides, throwing them up on the wall. Suddenly I felt hit as if by an arrow piercing my chest. I looked at my picture of a headstone in the peaceable, quiet cemetery in the Dutch settlement. Cows were grazing in the near distance. The headstone, with a sculpted little lamb, had a name on it, still legible. I walked up to the projected image to be able to decipher the name and then stopped. It was her name, the name of the mother who had died in labor and had left her husband bereaved. She had disappeared from view only to reappear through this silent marker on her grave. I stood in tears, overcome by emotion, as if grieving for a family member that I had lost. The photograph, taken almost casually as one of a series, had forever changed meaning. It had inserted itself into my quasi-familial identification with a family far away in time and space. I decided to make this experience part of the story I would tell the next day. It would serve to give the audience a sense of my personal involvement in a community history that I wished to explore with their help. As it turned out, I managed to convince many of them of my bona fides and to persuade them to open their private archives and their stores of memories to me. Often there was a reciprocity of services involved. Many had diaries, sets of letters, and other documents that were in Dutch and which only I, through translation, could open for them.

At moments like these my family album begins to extend beyond the boundaries that my initial sense of a project had set. Audiences begin to expand beyond the small circle of viewers I originally had in mind. There were more such moments as time went on. As my own sense of exploring new territory began to wane, my gaze became more that of an American Studies scholar, aiming my camera at scenes and objects I wanted my students to see. At such moments, as much as in the case of my Dutch-American settlement project, my sense of an intended audience surpassed the boundaries of the family album. My gaze, at such moments, was filtered through academic interest, and sought illustrations in the context of an interpretation of American contemporary culture. When I photographed American shopping malls, commercial strips, Hoover Dam, the Kennedy Space Center, multilingual signs on streets and airports, neon-light commercial messages against a night sky, increasingly I had students in mind rather than my family.

Yet, throughout the album, one audience was always there. Faces of friends and their families appear throughout the collection, faces of my sons, faces of Sioe Kie, and now of Marianne. Yet the one audience I had in mind, in the final analysis, consisted of only one person: me. As I am writing this, in an apartment in Greenwich Village in New York, I look out my window, across a landscaped court, to apartments on the other side. It is early evening. Lights are on behind most windows. Tonight, as on previous nights, from one particular angle in my room there is an interplay between the leafless twigs of a tree, the frame of a window, a lampshade inside one room on the other side, that miraculously produces a radiant mask, like the face of the moon. Only this face is Sioe Kie's, a mask of yellowish light, yet lifelike. There is a detached, ironic smile. I'll try to photograph it. She has been watching me all along. What would she think of all this?

TWO ◉ PHOTOGRAPHY AND
IMMIGRATION

ONE INSPIRATION for this chapter has been my reading of the work of W. G. Sebald. The only way to characterize him is as a European writer. Born a German, he spent most of his adult life, until his untimely death in a car accident in 2000, in England. But more than his self-chosen location, it is his work that suggests the epithet of "European." The space that Sebald calls forth in his writing is a Europe without borders, open for the human power of recollection to roam, a space whose only map consists of the fragile lines of memory that his errant personae have left in their wake. His stories are all about the recovery of things past. The gaze of his characters takes in the objects of their surroundings only as markers of what has gone before, of life vanished. If there is a din of voices in his book, it is of voices long gone silent. While the stories may strike the reader as fables, as inventions, Sebald goes to great lengths to document his tales, to suggest factuality, by interspersing his text with photographs of European places, of characters in the stories, of documents that he tells us he has drawn on. At times, as in his haunting *Austerlitz,* the quest for lost memories results in the many fragments of recollection falling into a pattern, although puzzles remain. In other books the reader is left with just the fragments, at the end of a dizzying tour of a ghostly underworld where the past randomly springs to life only to vanish again in the dark.

In only one of his books, *The Emigrants,* does Sebald extend this imaginary realm to include American space.[1] But it is a space woven together by immigrants with a remembered European space. "I have barely any recollection of my own of Great-Uncle Adelwarth," reads the opening line of a story in which Sebald recounts his quest in search of an enigmatic uncle who left a lasting impression on the narrator on the one occasion when the uncle, along with other relatives who had migrated to the United States from the Weimar Republic, came over for a family reunion in the small southern German town where the narrator lived as a young boy. The American relatives' summer visits were, as the narrator tells us, the probable reason for his imaginary Americanization as an adolescent, roaming an imagined American space as "a venture in mimicry that was doomed to failure for various reasons that can easily be imagined." Yet, when he had given up on his American dreams as a student, he set sail for America "prompted by a photograph album of my mother's which had come into my hands a few months earlier and which contained pictures quite new to me of our relatives who had emigrated during the Weimar years." He meets those still alive, but the story is essentially one about his quest for the intriguing uncle who died years before. Slowly, piece by little piece, the deceased uncle comes to life through the many places where he lived, in Europe, in Egypt, in the United States. The narrator tells of a visit to the place where his uncle spent his last years, a sanatorium in upstate New York, no longer in use and in a state of disrepair, yet reconstructed through an act of imagination on the part of the narrator. In the end, though, the uncle remains elusive, a ghost only to be glimpsed briefly before vanishing again.

Reading the story, I was reminded of my own quest for the lives of emigrants long since dead. All a researcher has to go by are random traces left, such as letters sent home, photographs documenting their lives. Hardly ever is the record complete. Occasionally bits researched separately fall into place together. The exhilaration derives from re-creation, bringing back to life people whose pictures have disintegrated into disparate dots. Those rare moments resemble vicarious acts of filiopietism, like bringing back to life Great-Uncle Ambros Adelwarth.

In this chapter I propose to look at the ways in which immigrants in their new American setting kept up connections with relatives, friends, and neighbors in their areas of origin. They expressed these continuing bonds through letters sent home, trying to preserve a sense of intimacy with those who had stayed behind. They also added a touch of closeness through the use of photography as a visual aid providing vicarious eye contact. There is an enticing directness to these photographs, suggestive as they are of a density of information, even though their rich and manifold meanings to those beholding them at the receiving end may have faded after a century or more. All that later observers can do is to try to re-create the role of photographs in preserving virtual communities of intimacy spanning half the globe.

Those interested in American photography all know the great photographic icons of American immigration. They can, at the flick of a mental switch, call forth the images of immigrants setting foot on Ellis Island, carrying their meager belongings in a bundle. The images show, in a strange intimacy, the faces of immigrants, in repose, yet in anticipation of the imminent encounter with their new country. We may, among many examples, just mention Lewis Hine's "Madonna of Ellis Island," or Alfred Stieglitz's "The Steerage."[2] There have been millions of immigrants like those shown in such pictures, yet we have a sense of knowing them all and having shared their experiences. Photography has that strange power to catch the fleeting moment, while at the same time condensing into a single representation the great anonymous processes of history, with their casts of thousands if not millions, caught up in war, in migration, in industrialization, in urbanization. We look at these pictures and have a feeling of a "democratic vista" restored, of a meaningful communion reestablished with unknown and untold others. Neither they, nor their stories, are untold any longer. Photography, in its iconic powers, has the Whitmanesque force of a democratic art.

Much as photographic icons belong to the public domain, much as they have become public representations that powerfully control our collective imagination of vast and impersonal events, they are not unlike the individual human beings that they have frozen in their frames. Just as millions of unseen others hide behind the faces of those who we will never forget, so do millions of photographs lurk behind the glossy radiance of the pictures that have reached iconic status. They have not penetrated into the public domain. Nor for that matter were many of them ever intended to. They functioned always on a level of communication much more private than the pictures of Hine or Stieglitz, whose impulse was documentary, was precisely one of making a public statement. When

Stieglitz later reflected, in an almost transcendentalist vein, on what had moved him when he took the picture that would become known as "The Steerage," he said: "I saw shapes relating to one another—a picture of shapes, and underlying it, a new vision that held me: simple people, the feeling of ship, ocean, sky: a sense of release that I was away from the mob called rich." Private his emotion may have been, yet it was one of public communion, one moreover that he meant to turn into public communication. "Some months later, after 'The Steerage' was printed, I felt satisfied, something I have not been very often. When it was published, I felt that if all my photographs were lost and I were represented only by 'The Steerage,' that would be quite all right." This one single photograph then would have sufficed as Stieglitz's public statement, affirming his calling as an artist. It would forever "represent" him, through its very representation of an act of democratic communion.

But, as I said, most photographic representations of the immigrants functioned on a different level of communication. They were part of highly private exchanges, meant to convey their messages within private networks of relatives and friends. They added a visual element to ongoing written exchanges and could derive their precise reading only from that context. The icons that we all know how to read are like the photographs in the window display of an archive storing millions of pictures whose reading has become uncertain. It is an archive of almost Borges-like dimensions, a maze of many nooks and niches, stacked with uncataloged boxes of words and images, fragments of stories that we may no longer be able to piece together. Occasionally there are guides, ghostlike figures, who have only their memories to live by and who can bring words and pictures together again. One such guide emerges from the pages of Louis Adamic's *Laughing in the Jungle:* an old and frail return migrant from the United States to the old mother country, which, until recently, we knew as Yugoslavia. At one point Adamic remembers the day when as a young boy he sat beside this old man, listening to him, to his stories about work in the mines and the steel industry, looking at photographs that the old man had brought home with him—photographs of New York:

"The day before I sailed home I walked in the streets"—he pointed at the picture—"where the buildings are tallest—and I looked up, and I can hardly describe my feelings. I realized that there was much of our work and strength, frozen in the greatness of America. I felt that, although I was going home . . . I was actually leaving myself in America."[3]

But more often than not such explanatory voices have gone silent. We are left facing photographs that no longer tell their own story. We are no longer able to re-create the recognition they evoked at both ends of lines of communication maintained between immigrants and those who had stayed behind. Such photographs have become the silent documents of an anonymous past.

Thus, in the archives of the Historical Collection in Heritage Hall at Calvin College, Grand Rapids, the center of learning of the Christian Reformed Dutch-American community in the United States, the visitor comes upon many photographs whose sitters are referred to as "un-identified persons." Many of the older pictures are studio photographs, giving us the name of the studio in ornate lettering. The sitters have dressed for the occasion and are photographed against backdrops redolent of luxurious mansions. They were Stieglitz's "simple people" who briefly identified with "the mob called rich." Whom did these early immigrants want to impress? Were these photographs ever sent to relatives in the home country? Did they simply serve the purpose of an embellished family memoir, in their vicarious display of a life of ease and luxury?

We will never know. What we do know is that these photographs belong to an era and a genre of studio portraiture in which photography was made subservient to the creation of an illusion. The new mechanical medium reproduced for the many the pictorial aura of ease, refinement, and culture that only the wealthy could afford in the heyday of painting.* If this was democracy, it was the democracy of illusion. Costumes, stage props, and backdrops were all provided by the studio. Will-

---

*As regards this theme of the continuity from painterly traditions to conventions of representation in early photography, in the way that early automobiles were styled as if they were horse-drawn carriages., we are reminded of John Berger's comments in his *Ways of Seeing:* "Every image embodies a way of seeing. Even a photograph. For photographs are not, as is often assumed, a mechanical record. Every time we look at a photograph, we are aware, however slightly, of the photographer selecting that sight from an infinity of other possible sights" (John Berger, *Ways of Seeing* [Harmondsworth: Penguin Books, 1972], p. 10). And we may add that equally often it is the sitter's selection of a way of being seen, of self-representation. As for the more general theme of photography's continuity with painterly strategies of representation, Berger follows it through to present-day conventions of publicity photographs. In a similar vein Roland Barthes argues at one point that "La Photographie" (and he makes it sound as if it had a life and will of its own) "has been, and still is being tormented by the fantom of La Peinture. . . . It [the former] has turned the latter . . . into its ultimate and absolute Reference, paternal, as if it had been born from Painting" (Roland Barthes, *La Chambre Claire: Note sur la photographie* [Paris: Gallimard, Le Seuil, 1980], p. 55). There is a counterargument in Berger's book, though never fully pursued, of the radical changes that the

ingly the sitters subjected themselves to the choreographic rules and the stage directions that had modeled family paintings since the seventeenth century. The mold of self-presentation was definitely patriarchal, although it came in two varieties. Mostly, in the photographs where husband and wife are together, the husband is seated with his wife standing beside him. An extreme version of this choreography is a photograph of an old woman standing beside an empty chair. She was a widow. But in a sense the dead husband was still there, defining her role and position. Occasionally, though, the woman is seated, with the husband standing by her side, the good provider and protector in one. In the case of studio portraits of parents and their children, the parents are usually seated, with the children standing.

If these photographs show us reality as a fiction, it was not necessarily one consciously fabricated to mislead the friends and relatives back home in the mother country. The representational code underlying this particular genre of studio photography was widely known: this was what people, in Europe and America, expected portraits to look like. Yet the fact that people could have their pictures taken in the first place was proof, not only that they could afford this relative luxury, but also that even in their pioneer existence in America they could enjoy the amenities of a modern technical civilization. Studio photography was never far behind the frontier of settlement. Studio photographs were not solely a big-city phenomenon; many are the photographs taken in small towns all across the United States. For some it may have required a day trip to the nearest small town and back, yet the message was clear: civilization was never far. Theirs was not a life in the wilderness.

---

invention of the camera brought to established ways of seeing. "The camera isolated momentary appearances and in so doing destroyed the idea that images were timeless. Or, to put it another way, the camera showed that the notion of time passing was inseparable from the experience of the visual (except in paintings)" (p. 18). This is more in line with Walter Benjamin's ruminations on photography and the human sense of loss and imminent death. "What we know that we will soon no longer have before us," he writes—"this is what becomes an image" (Walter Benjamin, *Charles Baudelaire: A Lyric Poet in the Era of High Capitalism* [London: New Left Books, 1973], p. 87). The image bears witness to an experience that cannot come to light. The experience is the experience of the shock of experience, of experience as bereavement. This bereavement acknowledges what takes place in any photograph—the return of the departed. Although what the photograph photographs is no longer present or living, its having-been-there now forms part of the referential structure of our relationship to the photograph. In my opinion both themes, the one of photography's indebtedness to painting, and of the changes photography brought to our ways of seeing, should guide us in our reading of the early family photographs that immigrants sent home to loved ones.

Of course there were cases where the use of studio props did in fact serve the purpose of willful fabulation, where indeed the fictitious overstatement did go beyond the representational conventions that sitters and beholders shared in common. In his study of immigrants from the Italian Mezzogiorno, *Il pane dalle sette croste*, P. Cresci mentions a genre of studio photographs that showed the immigrants holding a bicycle or casually leaning on a motorcar.[4] More often than not these were the studio's property, used to convey an image of material well-being that may have been a distant dream to the immigrants as much as to their Italian relatives. Such photographs are a clear case of theatrical impression management. They were the visual accompaniment to the glowing overstatement in many of the immigrants' letters.

In general, whether or not the intended message was an overstatement, photographs were accompanied by words, either scribbled on their backs or in enclosed letters. Language served to add to the photographic information, contextualizing it by giving names, ages, color of eyes or hair, and by referring to the occasion, such as a baptism or a wedding anniversary. They were all matters of private relevance, providing the recipients with—literally—a closer look at their distant relatives and friends. Words were meant to add focus and detail to the photographic image, yet they could only function within the wider unspoken context of established relations of kinship or friendship. Outsiders, strangers to such intimate relationships, could never hope to get the full message. How much more strongly is this the case with later observers, such as students of immigration history: the passing of time and of generations has filtered if not erased family recollections, has caused the loss of letters and photographs, has severed the links that connected each meaningfully with the other. There has been a massive loss of vital context. We are left with the mere fragments of what once was a meaningful and ongoing communication across the Atlantic.

Yet the fragments are all over the place. The "archive" of immigration history is tentacular, reaching as far as the catchment area of American immigration. Letters and photographs, half-forgotten, half-remembered, are still being kept by individual families all across that area. Occasional conversations as much as concentrated research efforts can result in lucky strikes. Thus one day a Polish colleague, Jerzy Topolski, who spent a year with me at the Netherlands Institute for Advanced Research and who knew of my research interest, told me that he knew of photographs of distant relatives in late nineteenth-century America that were still being kept by family members in Poland. A little later in the year he brought them with him from Poland. They were all studio photographs, from Chicago and New York, all with the amber hue that tied them to the era of the "Brown Decade." There were more markers of time, place, and country of origin. In addition to the name and address of the studio, prominently featured below the actual picture, handwritten notes on the back added information of a more private nature. The notes were in Polish, but as Professor Topolski pointed out to me, it was a variety of Polish spoken in Silesia, with a clear admixture of Germanisms, such as literal translations of German words or German idioms. Thus, a simple message like "Son Joseph, 22 years old, 24th July 1896" gave away the region of origin: the phrase "22 years old," which runs parallel to German "22 Jahre alt" and which had exactly that same word order in the written Polish message, is not standard Polish. Similarly the word used for picture is a literal translation of the German word "Aufnahme" (which would translate into English as "recording"). Once again, the word strikes a contemporary Polish reader as a marker of Silesian Polish.

The brief notes at the time must have sufficed to put the various persons shown in the photographs unfailingly within a network of relatives living on both sides of the Atlantic. Such immediate genealogical mapping is no longer possible among their present-day offspring. The photographs are the faded effigies of relatives who themselves have faded from memory. No longer able to call forth a repertoire of anecdotes and stories and set in a context of silence, these photographs are not unlike weathered tombstones, the mute markers of family history. This comes out most tellingly in one of the Polish photographs. It is a portrait of a young woman showing just her head and shoulders, in the style of a sculptor's bust, the shape reduced to an oval, the rest retouched to nothingness. The impression is one of an image emerging in clear focus from an enveloping mist. The little photograph was taken by Hartley's Studio in Chicago. The name is partly hidden from view by some of the flowers and leaves of an ornate wreath that encircles the little picture. For in fact, what we are looking at is a photograph of a photograph, once again taken by the Hartley Studio. Below the wreath there is a rectangular shape, suggesting the heavy stone lid of a grave. The whole is definitely a studio arrangement. More than any other photograph it conveys

"Forget me not." Photograph made in remembrance of a deceased family member. Private collection.

the sense of the past as lying irretrievably across the river Styx, in the domain of the dead. The handwriting on the back dryly informs us that the woman is Elisabeth. "When died she was 24 years, 3 months, and thirteen days old."

In a sense the other photographs are not that much different. They are all images of people that have long since died, regardless of what the handwriting tells us. "Son Joseph, 22 years old, 24th July 1896." A proud princelike Pole stares us in the face, a self-assured young man, dressed— or so it seems—for a night at the opera. "First communion," it says on the back of a photograph of a young girl. She wears an elaborate white dress; there is a flow of fine, white tulle covering her hair. Her left hand is at rest on a light, rattan stand; her right hand holds a church book. She looks us straight in the face, her life ahead of her. "Granddaughter Gertruda Pallow, daughter of Franzisek. She was 4 years old in January 1896"—a photograph of a darling young girl, dressed like a little princess, that was sent to her grandmother in Poland. The picture is all that the grandmother may ever have seen of the girl, frozen for all time at age four. None of these other photographs has been wreathed and rephotographed the way the picture of Elisabeth was; they were never intended to carry a message of death, yet to us they have the same quality of a memento mori. The passing of time has placed them irrevocably in that genre.

Only the living memory of those beholding a photograph can bring the sitters back to life. I was reminded of this when reading a story by James Schaap, a Dutch-American author.[5] The story tells us of a young man who has come to see his grandmother on her deathbed. He enters the bedroom. "Nameless faces lined the walls, and an old Dutch couple peered at me from an ornate oval frame hung above the headboard. I always loved that room, for there was excitement here, the fascination of experiences long past. I loved to sneak in as a boy, to sit alone on the bed and look around." Now, for the first time, he is not alone. In her final days, his grandmother tells him about the past before it is too late, about "the nameless faces" on the wall, her father and mother. "What was your mother like, Grandma? Like you?" Slowly, in answer to his queries, she brings the past back to life, telling a story that she had kept to herself for years, about a disastrous fire on board an immigrant ship, crossing Lake Michigan en route to Sheboygan. The father died, fighting the fire; the mother died looking for one of her daughters. The portrait of his grandmother's parents comes to life: "I glanced at the portrait. I had seen it often before. It had come from Grandma's uncle in Holland. He was seated on a chair as big as a throne, his wife's hand rested on his shoulder as she stood soberly at his side." And as the drama unfolds, of his grandmother's parents dying but also of his grandmother going back in time, reviving the story, the grandson keeps looking up at the picture. "I tried to imagine [them] as Grandma spoke." They are no longer nameless faces.

When I was reading the story, there was a strange sense of déjà vu, of something half-forgotten pushing to resurface. Suddenly, there it was. In a book by a Dutch amateur historian, in which he pieces together the emigration histories of his forebears, reference is made to the same tragic event on Lake Michigan. I had heard the story before and had gone through the same emotions as the young man in Schaap's story listening to his grandma. I had also been looking at photographs of people who had been in the fire. They were reproduced in the book, relatives and friends of relatives of the author. In his act of filiopietism, he manages to draw outsiders like me into a quasi-familial circle, where "nameless faces" are being restored to their place in history through stories told by their distant offspring.[6]

If, in the exchanges between immigrants and their relatives and friends in the home country, photographs acquired their full meaning and sense only in a context of written words, one of two things usually happens with the passing of time. Either we find separate photographs that time has cut loose from their accompanying annotation, or we are left only with the annotation, with cryptic references in letters to pictures that originally must have been enclosed. Many are the people who in acts of filiopietism have sat down to collect and order what is left of the communications of their relatives across the Atlantic. They have sorted out such letters as have remained; they have made copies available to official immigration archives in their home countries or in the United States. But more often than not these are the mere fragments of exchanges that went on for years if not decades.

One of the tasks that immigration research has set itself is archival. It is precisely the task of bringing together as many of these fragments as one possibly can. And the results have been impressive. Massive amounts of immigrants' letters have been collected, ordered, and made available for research. Large selections have been published, in the United States and in the main countries of emigration in Europe.[7] Larger collections are available in immigration archives in all those countries. Yet much of the archives are still as labyrinthine as before. Serendipity still reigns supreme; researchers in the field keep stumbling upon unmined treasures. No single researcher can claim to have seen it all, or can confidently say to have gone over a representative sample. Yet there is always the temptation to come up with some tentative general statements. So, with all due provisos, let me give some general impressions before I go into greater detail.

My own work in immigration history has been concentrated mostly on Dutch immigrants in the United States and Canada.[8] In the course of my research I have come upon hundreds, if not thousands, of letters, and there are new finds all the time. On that basis, and also on the basis of such collections of letters as have been published in other countries, it seems safe to say that photographic information played only a marginal role. Entire exchanges between family members, no matter if they went on for decades, have no reference at all to photographs. A collection of Dutch immigrants' letters published by Herbert J. Brinks never once mentions photographs in its selected fragments.[9] And only a few of the many photographic illustrations in the book are clear cases of pictures sent home to the mother country. Thus, there is one example of those stilted studio photographs that we have already described as a genre. We see husband and wife, the man sitting, the woman standing by his side, both looking as if they have just swallowed a broomstick. The caption, in quotation marks, reads: "In this letter I send you my portrait and that of my husband. I can also send you the children, but then it may be a little too heavy." Another picture, from about 1906, is taken outdoors, on an unpaved street, with a group of people posing alongside a hearse. According to the legend, the photograph was taken on the occasion of the burial of a young immigrant in Grand Rapids and was intended for his mother in the Netherlands. This photograph is more in the vein of documentary reportage than the highly stylized studio picture of the deceased Polish woman, yet again the photographic image served to document one of life's irreversible moments, like birth, like baptism, like death. . . .

One explanation for the relative scarcity of visual images in the letters that Herbert Brinks used, or in most of the letters that I myself have worked with, may have to do with religion. After all, these are letters from a staunchly Calvinist immigrant population that tends to conceive of itself as the people of the Word, averse to any form of visual representation. For these descendants of the iconoclasts, these worshippers in whitewashed churches devoid of imagery, the mechanical muse of photography may have been just another idol. Yet, irrespective of religion, the relative scarcity of written references to enclosed pictures is too widespread for this explanation to hold.

To the extent that we find photographs mentioned at all in immigrants' letters, what does this tell us about their communicative value and function? Let us consider a few examples. For the very early period in the history of photography I have one set of letters, exchanged between members of the Te Selle family, and ranging in time from 1865 to 1911. The earliest mention of a photograph is in a letter from 1869, scribbled in the margin and added almost as an afterthought: "Here is a protrait [*sic*] of our little Dela. She is now eleven months old. She sits on a chair but it was difficult to keep her still for so long." Another note in the margin adds this: "I took the letter to the post office but then it was too heavy. I will send the protrait with G. Lammers." In a letter sent from Winterswijk in the Netherlands in 1873 to relatives who also lived in the Netherlands, there were originally two enclosures: a letter from an elderly uncle in America and his photograph. In the little accompanying note we read: "So I send you this letter, and also the portrait, so you can see him on it, and also read in this letter how he is doing. Also you can perhaps send it to your other sister who would also like to have it and see it." In June 1873, the same old uncle writes a long letter, again from Holland, Sheboygan County, Wisconsin. Following a pious dissertation— "And Blessed are we if we hear, do and maintain what God says in his word. But also we know that there is an other, who is called Devil, Satan, Old Snake, the Seducer, Lord of Darkness, God of this, our century . . ."—there are a few bits of news, about a granddaughter marrying, about the weather. And then, in spite of the orthodox, old-Calvinist exposé, there is this line: "Also I feel the urge to send you the portrait of my Deceased Wife; we had only one portrait of my wife, and this very same one we had duplicated which we now send you." Again his nephew in the Netherlands passes the letter and the portrait on to his uncle's sister and brother-in-law. "The portrait is yours to keep," he adds.

In 1883 there is a reference to a different kind of visual information, not a portrait of a family member, but a picture of a wind-driven water pump. "This autumn we had a water wind pump put on our well. Now we don't have to draw the water for the cattle ourselves any more. It cost a hundred dollars. Here on this little print you see its picture." Then, in a letter of October 1892, there is the anxious query for an acknowledgment of receipt: "On February 2 this year I have sent all the potrets [*sic*] of my children and of my son-in-law with the request to write back soon, but then later on we got a letter from you which made me conclude that you hadn't received it. Then I have done it again once more but if they have gone lost again at sea I don't know." Apparently the enclosure of photographs must have been an act of great significance, worthy of repetition and the cause of worried inquiry.

This one collection of thirty-five letters, spanning a total of forty-seven years, is fairly representative of other such correspondence. The references to photographs are few, and most of those are related to portraits. Apparently, the main informative function of photographic enclosures was to maintain a sense of visual proximity among family members in spite of geographic distance. This sense is vividly evoked in a letter sent from Santa Monica, California, to Leeuwarden in the Dutch province of Friesland: "Dear nephew, I have received 'in good order' the photographs that were passed on to me from Yakima. After I had received your letter I looked forward eagerly to seeing them and so, as you can understand, it made an unusual impression on me 'to see' a likeness[10] of my next of kin. After such a long absence. Your mother I could not recognize as the sister whom I had pictured in my 'memory.' Her appearance, it seemed to me, had changed. Your father seemed to me more or less the same as I remembered him. A little older but the same 'jovial' person. I value the possession of the photographs and thank you for the interest and 'attention to send them tot mij' [note the characteristic blend of English and Dutch]."[11]

Pictures of inanimate matter—of the natural scene, objects, for instance, or machinery (such as the windmill referred to above), or the built-up environment—hardly figure at all in immigrants' letters. Such photos are more likely to show up in business-related correspondence or publications. Thus the Noord-Amerikaansche Hypotheekbank (the North American Mortgage Bank), operating from Leeuwarden, the capital of the province of Friesland, with representatives in Dutch immigration centers of North Yakima, Washington, and Bozeman, Montana, produced an advertisement folder with two photographs and the following two captions: "Picking apples in one of the valleys in Washington" and "Harvest and threshing combine at work in Eastern Washington." It also gave the names of its two representatives in the United States. Clearly people looked at such visual information with different eyes, with a view to business opportunities and migration possibilities. And, of course, there were many channels conveying precisely such information: shipping lines, land development corporations, migration societies. But that was not the information that people expected to be carried by the much more private lines of communication that connected friends and family members across the Atlantic.

Clearly, in the early years both of photography and of large-scale Dutch migration, economic considerations affected the selective nature of photographic information as well. Having portraits made and sending them across the ocean was relatively costly. A letter from Michigan City, Indiana, dated June 5, 1894, is quite explicit on this point: "Had we not had such a bad time, we would have had our pictures taken this summer: but now this will have to wait a while." Yet, economic means permitting, the first priority in the exchange of pictures was family portraits rather than any other topic of visual information. Our same correspondent, in a later letter sent from Holland, Michigan, in the year 1900, is exultant: "Dear Brother and Sister, With joy and gratitude we received your letter with portrait. We were overjoyed for now we could behold your family from afar: of Freerk we could not very well see that it werst thou. It is eight years hence since we saw each other."

Further evidence that this was the favorite subject of photographic information comes from a later period when price was no longer a limiting factor. When immigrants were better off, after years of hardship, and when photography itself had come within reach of the general public, family pictures were still by far the leading genre. Rather than economics it was now the technology of the early amateur cameras that set the constraints. Exposure time practically prevented indoor photography. But even outdoors the light was not always sufficient. "Last Sunday we have taken pictures of the children. We would take a few more the next Sunday but it was a dark day so we have to wait until the following Sunday. As soon as they are ready, we will send them to you. Monica is quite a girl already and Anna comes along nicely."

Photography had moved outside the confines of the studio and into the private realm of the family garden. If the focus was still on family members, explanatory notes now increasingly referred to details of the setting as well, such as "our house," "our front porch," "our garden patch." One caption reads: "This is our house, we built it." But still the eyes of the recipients of such pictures fastened most eagerly on the human presence. Tiny details of physical appearance were added in writing, or commented on in letters from the home country. Color of hair and eyes, signs of aging, family resemblances were standard topics in the exchanges accompanying this photographic communication. Photographs went from hand to hand among family members at the receiving end. "Dear cousin, . . . Have you received the portrait already of the little sisters? We sent six to aunt Klaasje; if you don't have them yet you can expect them every day now. Can you tell who they resemble? Not me, that much I can see myself." Or, in a letter from Chicago, written in the late 1920s by an American daughter-in-law married to a Dutch immigrant: "You all look so good on the picture, older of course but aren't we all getting older every day. Mother is much thinner but Dad he almost looks the same except for the grey hair."

In this later age of the amateur snapshot, there is a greater informality in the way people have themselves represented. People in their everyday clothes doing little chores around the house are a common theme: "Father feeding the chickens." Yet there are clear echoes of earlier strategies of self-representation. Often people still dress up for the occasion and stiffly pose for the photograph. The choreographies may be vaguely remembered and awkwardly executed, yet in the family groupings on the front porch we recognize the prescriptions and styles of self-representation that reigned supreme in the era of the studio photograph.

Yet another, highly practical function of photographic information is apparent in much post–World War II correspondence. Following the news of the wartime ordeal and of postwar scarcity in the Netherlands, immigrant relatives in the United States assumed the role of good providers. Many are the references in postwar correspondence to packages sent to the Netherlands of clothes, bicycle tires, and other goods that were in short supply. Long discussions of what kind of clothes would fit whom were a recurrent feature. In those discussions photography played its part, filling people in on such mundane matters as size and physical build. "Just imagine that I had thought Wiebe's size to be half-way between Pieter and Ulbe. That is why there was never anything his size in what I sent you." "Your mother is much more heavy-set than I am. Otherwise she is my size."

The photographs that we have considered were always of a highly private nature. They added to the exchange of intimate news between family members and close friends. They gave those at the receiving end a closer look at their correspondents and their immediate setting, their home, their garden, the street on which they lived. It was the closest possible technical approximation to an actual family reunion. And in fact family reunions taking place at the immigrants' end, when after two or three generations families had become dispersed across the United States, were a favorite item of photographic reportage to the old country.

Yet, playing their role within highly private networks, all such photographs were only one, highly specialized element in the transmission of visual images of the new country to those who had stayed behind. They represented only a slice of life, yet it was one that no other genre of photography could convey. There were always the varieties of public photography, published in weekly magazines and similar sources, which served as carriers of information about the United States. Yet another category of "official" photographic information was that put out by the Dutch government in the postwar period, when for the first time in the history of Dutch emigration the government adopted an official emigration policy in conjunction with the two main immigrant-receiving countries of the time, Canada and Australia. The Dutch government now acted as the main sponsor and coordinator of what had been an unplanned, voluntary process before. As one woman, married to a Dutch immigrant and living in Canada, remembered it: "[Her] husband came up with the idea to emigrate to Canada after seeing a large billboard, a piece of the Canadian government's recruitment propaganda." She described it as "a beautiful poster . . . a golden grainfield, waving in the breeze, with the obligatory happy and prosperous young emigrant family standing in the middle of it."[12]

Generation upon generation of immigrants have been drawn toward America under the impact of such public images, advertising the lures and attractions of the new country, casting America in the light of a land of promise and bounty. When confronted with the realities of American life, many must have felt a sharp disillusionment. As James Schaap tells us, in another of his tales of Dutch-American immigrant life: "De Kruyf had read about the scandals. He had seen the giant paintings of America when they had all lived in the old country. People from all over Europe had been cheated. He knew many who had come to this country with nothing but a picture from a lantern slide in their minds, thinking themselves somehow heirs to the riches of the new paradise." Collective experiences like these may have made the immigrants more distrustful of pictorial representations, may have made them more keenly aware of the conmanship behind much of the public imagery about America, yet in reaction the immigrants did not turn away from photography and its recording potential as such. If anything, they relied more on photographic records that they themselves produced and choreographed, for their own private use and that of their distant relatives in the old country. When we try to fathom the role played by family photographs, we should never lose this sense of context. The stories told by these highly private photographs, stored by family members in the home countries and circulated along with their letters among friends and relatives, were always private answers to the sobering reality of immigrant life. They offered as much a constructed, retouched, manipulated view of life in America as the pictures that circulated in the public realm. Yet they served a totally different psychological purpose. They could shore up the hopes and spirits of immigrants at times when their great expectations, fostered by one form or another of land development interests, threatened to collapse.

In "Sign of a Promise," the title story of the James Schaap collection,[13] there is a very moving vignette that beautifully illustrates this role and place of private photographs in the life of immigrants. The author takes us to the pioneer house of a Dutch-American family, struggling to survive on the prairie frontier in northwestern Iowa. They have recently moved there, in the restless search for success that had earlier taken them to Wisconsin and Minnesota. They are alone, the first in their part of the world to break the prairie soil. It has been raining for days, washing away the result of days of backbreaking work. The woman stands behind the window, looking out. "And the sky, spewing incessant rain, seemed to combine with the desert of grass to destroy whoever, whatever tried to exist there. The endless miles of prairie seemed to her a Godless expanse, and all the prayers she had learned as a child, no matter how loudly she could cry them to the heavens, could not bring her any closer to the God she had known in the old country. This land was so wide, so vast, so everlasting, that she felt her best prayers rise in futility, . . . to a God who had never minded this region of creation." Forlorn and forsaken, forgotten by a God who is normally the last hope and refuge for people of her religious background, the woman is in utter despair. "She turned from the window and looked back to the family portrait that hung on the mud wall. It had been taken in Wisconsin. She had wanted it immediately after their arrival in America to send to her parents in Holland, for she knew their concern and felt that they would be reassured by the clean faces and the Sunday clothes of the children. They knew very little of America. Some of the stories they had heard were like those of the land of Canaan—a land most bountiful, full of opportunity. But others were fearful, accounts of drought, storms, savages, violence, strange and horrid stories of people who didn't know the Lord. The family picture had helped, she knew, for it showed them tidy and happy, wearing the smiles that reflected the hopes and jubilation of a life filled with new opportunities. She knew they [her parents] would like it, for she liked it. This was the way she imagined things."

The last line is amazingly perceptive. It catches the meaning of photographs that immigrants had taken of themselves, presenting an ideal view of themselves to family members in the old country but, more important, to themselves as well. Family photographs in that sense are not pictures of the present, or records of the past; they are visions of the future. They document the hopes and anticipations of immigrants as they themselves harbored them, not those conjured up by outside interests. If the latter are a reservoir of disappointment and despair, the former are the repertoire of hope.

For a wide variety of reasons, then, photographs have continued to play their role as a source of private information, for the earlier immigrant families as much as for those who left the Netherlands in the tens of thousands in the postwar period. Emigration from the Netherlands began to taper off in the late 1950s, at precisely the time when the Dutch national economy began to gather steam. Then, with prosperity coming to the mother country, along with the technological revolution in international travel facilities, a final ironic twist occurred in the role of photography as a means of private communication. All those amateur historians of family migration who did not themselves migrate, who in fili-opietistic enthusiasm have husbanded the store of information, of letters and photographs, who have typed out the letters and arranged the photographs neatly in albums, have one final surprise for the researcher who has come to see them. There are likely to be those few final pages in the picture album where the researcher recognizes his host amidst his distant American relatives. One looks at one's host and points at the picture: "That's you there!" The host nods in agreement. Yes, he has gone across the ocean, not as an immigrant, but as a tourist. He has decided to close the circle and go see for himself. Yet the reunion with family members, whose memories have been kept alive over the years through his loving, archival work, is a memorable event in its own right. It is worthy of the same medium of photography that kept earlier generations connected, in an age when emigration appeared to be a definite farewell.

 PUBLIC IMAGES

THREE ◉ THE HISTORY OF
PHOTOGRAPHY AND THE
PHOTOGRAPHY OF HISTORY

The Afterlife of Photographs

IN THE EMERGENCE of mass culture, in Europe and the United States, one momentous change was the shift in cultural communication away from words, printed or spoken, toward images. Of course, in earlier centuries the mass of the illiterate had been exposed to pictorial imagery with a view to their cultural incorporation. The Catholic Church in particular had provided extensive and elaborate picture shows in their stained glass windows, their paintings and frescoes, and lush sculptural displays. If this was mass exposure to images, it was mostly a matter of exposure during mass. The Reformation, though, with its Calvinist ethos and the rise of the capitalist spirit, had signaled the advent of a cultural hegemony that emphasized the word and mass literacy and, often in literal iconoclasm, had smashed the centrality of images and the mass idolatry they were considered to sustain. Henceforth, in the area in northwestern Europe and North America where this cultural hegemony held sway, pictorial—or ideographic—forms of communication gave way to a worldview centered on language and its conceptual and analytic rigor. However, to the extent that the Reformation, and more generally the Renaissance, had given greater centrality to individuals as the agents of history, pictorial representation survived to celebrate their new position on the stage of history. Paintings in this age became a reflection of the spirit of individualism in a dual sense. They were the work of individual artists rather than of anonymous craftsmen. They were also the public representation and projection of the individual success and social status of their owners, or of the collective secular prowess of mercantile city states and republics, such as Venice or the Dutch republic. Thus, there was a circulation of images—among elite circles, and in the public domain of secular societies—yet they reflected the taste of established social elites. Forms of representational art fulfilled their communicative functions in ways that reaffirmed rather than undermined the social order. Art was assigned its place on the level of high culture and found its market among a clientele that was at the high end of the social pyramid.

However, as Joseph Schumpeter famously pointed out in the early twentieth century, capitalism is an engine of creative destruction. It is never long before its restless inventiveness and quest for profitability reshuffle the pack of established social practices and relations. Similarly with established cultural practices. Hegemonic views, elevating the word over the image or establishing art at the high end of the cultural hierarchy, came up against the unsettling implications of a vast array of technical inventions in the area of mechanical reproduction. All of these, in the logic of their nature, catered to markets that, if anything, we would have to call mass markets. Thus, the Gutenberg revolution, which introduced mechanical printing, from its incipience conjured up a mass market of literate readers. These implications may long have been contained, yet with the rise of literacy and of ideas of popular sovereignty and democracy the printing press was the first of many devices of mechanical reproduction to create and cater to a mass market. A similar revolution came later to the world of images. Most prominent among the inventions that brought this revolution was photography.

It may seem ironic, but the invention of photography—of a machine able to "write with light"—did not initially give rise to cultural resistance on such grounds as the mechanical reproduction of images and their mass circulation. In the early years an aura of mystery and wonder, as well as of uniqueness, enveloped daguerreotypes, the first form of photography. Only when looked at from the right angle did an image spring forth, ghostlike, fleetingly, as if from a realm of darkness. There was a sacral element in photography's potential to capture and freeze instantly what to the human eye and mind was always in flux, in motion. For the more pedestrian qualms about images circulating in relative autonomy, beyond the control and auspices of cultural guardians, we have to look elsewhere. In the early years of wonder at the marvel of photography, it would have been hard to project a later age when cameras would be like natural appendages of tourist bellies. There was, however, a parallel invention that almost from the start elicited a response of cultural concern, if not denigration. It was the invention of chromolithography in the early nineteenth century. Like photography, chromolithography was invented in Europe before it traveled to the United States. Its mechanics and purpose were never shrouded in mystery. It aimed at the simple, straightforward reproduction, in color, of man-made images. From its incipience it was practical, down-to-earth, and openly showed its colors as a tool aiming at a mass market. Thus, more than photography, it directly addressed elite concerns about the hallowed aura of high art, and prompted an elite discourse defending and defining the kind of educated public that could properly appreciate artistic renditions of the world.

Between 1840 and 1900 original paintings were being reproduced lithographically in color and sold in America by the millions. At the peak of America's Victorian era, the mass-produced color lithograph waved unchallenged as the flag of popular culture. Its pervasiveness, as Peter Marzio points out, has led some historians to see the fifty-year period following the Civil War as the "chromo-civilization."[1] And, as he continues to say, "[t]he most compelling aspect of this story . . . is that the chromo civilization was marked by a faith in fine art, a belief in the power of art to enrich the life of anyone. This attitude embraced the notion, heretical to some, that fine art should be reproduced, packaged, and offered to the masses. The chromo embodied this attitude—it was the democratic art of the post–Civil War decades." Yet there were those, public intellectuals among them, who begged to differ.

The man who, in 1874, coined the phrase "chromo-civilization" as a pejorative term was Edwin Lawrence Godkin, editor of the weekly magazine *The Nation*, a publication that the famous English observer James Bryce described as the "best weekly not only in America but in the world."[2] In the opinion of Godkin, the chromolithograph was the quintessence of the democratization and, therefore, debasement of high culture. It represented a "pseudo-culture," being one of a plethora of evil media, newspapers among them, that "diffused through the community a kind of smattering of all sorts of knowledge, a taste for 'art'—that is, a desire to see and own pictures—which, taken together, pass with a large body of slenderly equipped persons as 'culture,' and give them an unprecedented self-confidence in dealing with all the problems of life, and raise them in their own minds to a plane on which they see nothing higher, greater, or better than themselves." Echoing a long-ranging historical critique of mass culture as it emerged along with mass society, from Alexis de Tocqueville to Walter Benjamin and Daniel Boorstin (think of the latter author's disparaging views of the "pseudo event" in his 1962 study, *The Image*[3]), Godkin saw the chromolithograph as a cheap copy of a beautiful oil painting, destroying for the viewer the specialness of the original (or, as Walter Benjamin would have it, its "aura"[4]). To public intellectuals and culture critics like Godkin, any culture that was packaged and ready for purchase was by that token deeply suspect. The chromo, according to Godkin, led to the creation of "pick-up" culture and to the tyrannical hold of external appearances on the masses. Culture would become entirely exteriorized and would turn into a thin veneer. True civilization, to Godkin, was less concerned with the dissemination of culture or with an exploration of what a democratic art, in a Whitmanesque vein, could possibly be, and more dedicated to the pursuit of truth: it was the product of an internal force, "the result of a process of discipline, both mental and moral." It was something spiritual and intellectual, formed by labor and self-denial. It was, in fact, elitist.

This demanding view of civilization may strike readers as typical more of a European cultural discourse than of an America in search of a truly democratic art, and therefore as less likely to hold sway in America, which would be more welcoming to technical devices, such as mechanical reproduction, that would make for mass production, distribution, and consumption of cultural goods. Voices and views such as Godkin's may stand in a long line of elite resistance in America to culture produced for the many rather than the few, yet they have always come from a beleaguered minority whose cultural anguish took its cues from European elites, far more solidly entrenched and assured of their cultural hegemony. In America the odds were stacked against such views in radically different ways. If, in counterdistinction to this continued orientation toward European cultural standards and views, there was a clearly American voice, it daringly spoke on behalf of an American culture whose single purpose and mission it was to be democratic. Therefore, whatever capitalism's inherent potential for creative destruction, working on both sides of the Atlantic, America's cultural climate made for a far greater willingness to explore capitalism's innovations as so many promises for the democratization of culture.

It was not long after its invention that photography developed in ways that much more radically showed its promise as a technical tool for the mass circulation of images. Chromolithography was in fact never more than a technique solely for the reproduction of images handmade by individual craftsmen. Photography was much more radically modern, much more representative of an emerging technical civilization, in the sense that the very images it produced relied on technical contraptions, such as the camera and light-sensitive emulsions. The very production of photographic images was mechanical. In its early years photography's radically modern nature could still be contained within cultural conventions that saw the individual photograph essentially in the light of painterly productions, produced in studios and displayed in portrait galleries. Relentless technical development of the new medium would soon make for the reproducibility of photographic images on a massive scale and for their commercial distribution among a mass audience. Only then, in this stage of the mass circulation of photographic images, did Americans, in a mixture of technical and commercial prowess, enthusiastically organize the markets for the consumption of images, inducing a mass craving for images, while at the same time satisfying it. European countries were among the early pioneers but often saw their own markets taken over, if not actually organized and served, by American entrepreneurial energy later on. It is a history not unlike that of film in the 1920s.

The first mass-cultural form of photography was the stereograph, supplying viewers with three-dimensional pictures of places and people they would never likely see with their own eyes. The marvel of this medium was that it not only froze time, as all photographs do, but also caught space in a time warp. Viewers were confronted with a virtual space of uncanny realism where the eye could wander, yet this space was as inaccessible as the past itself. In the years before further technical developments such as rotogravure allowed for the reproduction of photographs in newspapers and illustrated magazines like the *National Geographic,* stereograph companies produced a vast visual inventory of the world. Stereographs were produced as early as the 1850s, but not until the development of gelatin emulsions and mass production techniques in the 1880s did they become as ubiquitous as television today. In their early days stereographs were produced in virtually every country that had commercial photographers. The first major producer was the London Stereoscopic Company, established in 1854. Intent on making its advertising slogan, "No home without a stereoscope," a reality, it sold over a million views in 1862. The Parisian company of Ferreir almost equaled that sales figure in the same year. But by the late nineteenth century stereographs had become primarily an American phenomenon, exported from its mass market to the smaller national markets of Europe. In 1900 there were 6,000 stereograph publishers in the United States and only 1,500 in Europe. The two largest stereograph companies, the Keystone View Company and Underwood & Underwood, published magazines for home consumers, teachers' manuals, salesmen's publications and "scientific" articles on the unique role stereographs had in educating and informing Americans about the world. At the same time, such activities testified to the marketing acumen of Americans. The American publishers issued an estimated five to seven million *different* images before the last stereograph company stopped manufacturing them in the late 1930s.

Unlike images circulating in public space—posters, advertisements, or pictures in newspapers and magazines—stereographic images, produced and distributed en masse, in the end made for a highly private consumption. In the privacy of individual homes, people could now set out on imaginary journeys, acquainting themselves with worlds otherwise far beyond their physical horizons. Thus stereographs allowed Americans mentally to roam across the vast expanse of their own country, caught up as it was in restless exploration and development. This served to instill a sense of participation in the larger national enterprise and to reinforce a sense of national citizenship, a view of America as an "imagined community." Furthermore, in the view of a larger world outside America, stereographs confirmed people in America, and more generally the West, in their conventional ideas of cultural superiority, of belonging to an advanced civilization carrying everything before it in its relentless march across the globe. Even where the photographer's impulse was documentary, as in the case of Edward Curtis's huge project to portray American Indians in the Far West, there was the implied meaning that what his photographs showed were native cultures doomed to disappear. He himself captioned one of his photographs—four Indians on horseback riding away from the viewer toward a darkened sky, the first one turning his head and looking back at the viewer—"The vanishing race." Among Europeans, though, stereographs may have had the further impact of disseminating a view of America as the advance force in establishing the global hegemony of Western civilization. In their view America came to be seen as having stolen a march on Europe in the process of modernization. Stereographic views of America's natural wonders, of its cities, its industry, its vitality and energy, must have left people in awe at what we might call an American sublime.[5] These views established in the European mind a sense of America as forming the pinnacle of Western civilization.

If stereographs sat astride the divide between public mass production and the private consumption of images (albeit a consumption on a mass scale), a huge further step in merging the public and the private in the mass circulation of images was the introduction of the Kodak camera. As a technical contraption the device was typically American in a number of ways. It combined production techniques of replaceable parts; it aimed at user-friendliness and, most important, at democratizing the tool of photography. Everyone could henceforth be his or her own photographer. Press the button and Kodak would do the rest. As the French slogan had it: "Click, clack, merci Kodak." On a mass scale, photography would henceforth allow individuals to record their own individual lives, catching highly private moments with a view to producing visual archives of individual memories, "family albums." All the way from production to consumption, photography had now entered the realm of the private and domestic. As for the mass dissemination of this new tool, one further element struck Europeans as typically American: the marketing acumen through advertising that Americans displayed in creating a demand for the Kodak camera, in Europe as well as in the United States.

Entire areas of human communication—across generations, within families when they wished to relive their own histories, or across geographic distance as in the case of immigrants informing those who had stayed behind[6]—had henceforth become connected to visual exchanges through the miracle of photography. Millions of photographic images, taken by individuals for individual consumption, have come to constitute a vast archive of visual memories. It offers dramatic testimony to the way in which photography has affected the human need to remember. It testifies to an almost magical exercise: to prevent time from eroding the visual features of a past that once was our present.

Much as photography may have entered the private sphere as a memory tool, its role in the public sphere was undiminished. In the mass circulation of public images photography reached a new stage when technical developments made for the instant transmission of images across the globe. It meant a sea change in the way that people now conceived of current events. The writing press would henceforth have to make room for colleagues wielding a camera rather than a pen. As a result a new genre of journalism emerged, known as photojournalism. From the 1920s, in both Europe and the United States, the illustrated press got a new lease of life, replacing older forms of visual representation, such as engravings, with photographs, hoping to satisfy a public need for visual realism. A new form of reportage emerged, known as the photo essay, in which photographs told a story and such text as remained served only as a verbal guide to the correct "reading" of the images.

Like the stereograph before, photojournalism in the 1920s came to serve as a vehicle for the transmission of American images to Europe, catering to a public eager to see more of a country and a culture that was flooding Europe with vibrant new forms of mass entertainment and leisure-time pursuits. Leading photo magazines in Europe, in addition to printing American photographs, sent their own photographers to report on the New World and to capture the otherness of a different culture, familiar yet utterly alien. There were famous photographers among them. Thus, the *Berliner Illustrierte Zeitung* sent Erich Salomon over on several assignments to catch "Strange America," the title of the first of his photo stories.[7] One way for Salomon to capture the "American way of life" was to focus on everyday aspects unfamiliar to his audience yet confirming established, if not stereotypical, views of America as a country balancing precariously between a daring modernity and a mechanization of life that threatened to reduce individuals to cogs in a machine. His witty study of an American self-service restaurant—"Non-Stop Dining"[8]—is typical of his style. The pun on dining in the German title—*Essen am laufenden Band*—alludes not only to voraciousness (one translation could be "eating continuously") but also to mass production ("food from the assembly line"). In a series of five staged photographs he appears as the uninitiated outsider who sits down at a table, waiting to be served. Captions add a minimal dialogue in which the waitress introduces him to the style of the American self-service restaurant. Of course, this has all come to Europe later, but as in so many other instances this first European encounter with a particular aspect of the thoroughgoing rationalization of life cast it in the light of something typically American.[9] Europeans chose to be both stunned and fascinated as well as haughtily amused if not worried by what they called "Americanism." If the word anti-Americanism applies to these interwar years, it is in the sense of a rejection of this type of Americanism. If America at the time seemed to augur the European future, Europeans were of two minds about it. They liked the prospect of prosperity through mass production, yet feared the specter of mediocrity and cultural leveling through standardization.

If photographs in our discussion so far have appeared as just another mass cultural medium, it is time to return to the concerns about a chromo-civilization, that is, to concerns about a mass circulation of images as mere visual entertainment. The visual overload of contemporary society was seen as a poor substitute for the traditional, verbal flow of information and as a threat to the idea of the well-informed citizen. But photography, as pioneered by Americans, was never solely used as a tool for mass communication, subservient to commercial purposes. Americans have also been pioneers in establishing photography as art. Against a facile rejection of the new medium as capable of nothing more than producing mechanical images, requiring no craftsmanship or creative talent, they set artistic standards and produced a body of work that lifted the new medium to a level where the camera, like the painter's brush, was nothing more than a tool in the hands of creative artists. A leading American voice in this struggle for the emancipation of photography was that of Alfred Stieglitz around the turn of the nineteenth century. But photographers before him had already struck Europeans by the fine quality of their work, particularly as regards the artistry of their prints. As early as the 1867 Paris International Exhibition, Europeans were impressed by the American landscape photographs. There Carleton E. Watkins exhibited twenty-eight large prints and three hundred stereographs. There were also California landscapes by George S. Lawrence and Thomas Houseworth, which were praised in the *Illustrated London News*. Subsequently Watkins received a gold medal and Thomas Houseworth a bronze medal for their achievements. Hermann Vogel, a photography juror representing Prussia for the exposition, a photographic chemist and scholar, and later Alfred Stieglitz's photography professor, summarized it nicely: "America is still to us a new world, and anything which gives us a true representation as a photograph, is sure to be looked upon with wondering eyes."[10] His views would be echoed by later Europeans who with astonishment discovered that America, though not a traditional *Kulturnation* like Germany, had something artistically valuable to offer. Thus, on the occasion of the First International Amateur Exhibition of photography, held in Hamburg, Germany, in 1893, one reviewer expressed himself thus: "Probably nobody would have expected the Americans to be the most noble and refined group—in their artistic expression and their appearance in the whole exhibition. After all there seems to be a strong and original artistic movement in this young *Kulturnation*."[11] The tradition of fine printing, of the photograph as an object of beauty, has a long history in the United States, and was only further confirmed through the teaching of grandees such as Edward Weston and Ansel Adams, and other photographers from the Group f/64 who advocated straight photography. Their intent was, in the words of a manifesto drawn up by Ansel Adams, to keep the medium "independent of ideological conventions of art and aesthetics that are reminiscent of a period and culture antedating the growth of the medium itself."[12]

But for new mechanical art forms such as photography or film to establish themselves firmly, more was needed than a small circle of mutual admiration societies. A whole artistic infrastructure was required, with universities offering programs in photography, museums and galleries willing to buy and exhibit the work of individual photographers, and a critical community publishing in photography journals. In all these areas America has led the way. As Jean Kempf points out, it was not until the 1970s that the realization dawned on the French that the photograph was an aesthetic object in its own right and that there was such a thing as an artist-photographer. According to him, it would take another decade or so for this awareness to have practical consequences for the infrastructure. French photographers such as Henri Cartier Bresson may have enjoyed worldwide fame, but first and foremost as photojournalists. Their view of photography, as summed up in the preface of Cartier-Bresson's 1953 *Images à la sauvette,* was of the photograph recording an *objective* outside reality. The Americans brought the French the idea of a *photographic* reality, of the photographic *object* replacing the emphasis on *subject* matter.[13] Tellingly, the place of some of Europe's great photographers in the pantheon of art photography was secured by the early recognition of their work by American colleagues. In the case of Eugène Atget, for instance, it was Berenice Abbott who in Paris collected his work and promoted it in the United States.

If the American pioneering role in the emancipation of photography as a new form of art is remarkable, equally striking is the European sense of surprise and amazement. European preconceived ideas of American culture as intrinsically incapable of producing anything artistically worthwhile, at least as measured by European yardsticks, were given the lie. What is strikingly absent from the American debate about photography as art are any self-conscious considerations of an American cultural deficit. Never, in the field of photography, did Americans anxiously follow the European scene or did they await cues from Paris or other European cultural capitals, as they have done in so many other areas of artistic production. At least in this new area of a mechanical art they were unburdened by any sense of cultural inferiority.

How remarkable then that in another similar area, that of film, developments took a different course. Again, in the years following World War I, America took the lead. But it did so in ways that in the eyes of Europeans seemed to confirm rather than upset their stereotyped views of American culture. Film production in America unabashedly geared itself to the mass market with production techniques that seemed to follow an industrial rather than an artistic logic. In the European attempts at saving film as another potential art form from the pressures of the mass market, intellectuals and culture critics were quick to conceive of films coming from America as a negative yardstick, a model to be avoided rather than followed. One reason for this difference between the artistic evolution of photography and film may have to do with the economics of film production. Compared with the production of individual fine prints of artistic photographs, the organization of film production involves many people and much money. In conquering markets, domestically and abroad, Americans were never loath to follow the dictates of a mass market. In terms of intellectual debate concerning the status of film as art they were never as quotable as in the area of photography. That they were instrumental in democratizing the new medium at the same time, managing to find a mass audience for film as mass culture, while upsetting established discourses concerning high versus low culture, was a thing that would dawn on European critics only much later.

Iconic Photographs and Their Afterlife

Why is it that photographs have a power of epic concentration, condensing larger moments in history into one iconic image? The quest for an answer takes us back to earlier reflections in this book on the way the human mind stores arresting moments. Psychologists in their use of the metaphor of "flashbulb memories" suggest an analogy between pictures of the mind—photographs taken by the human eye—and the medium of photography. The power of iconic photographs derives precisely from our feeling that such photographs have done the work of memory for us. They have an impact on the human mind similar to what our eyes would have done, had we been present. They produce "flashbulb memories" for us, turning us into vicarious witnesses, irrespective of distance and time. The effect has critically to do with what one student of the medium has called "le silence sauvage de la photographie," the savage silence of photographs.[14] They speak no words, use no rhetorical flourish, no linguistic embellishments or evasions. They freeze transient motion into lasting stillness. Neither film nor television footage has this power of silence. Stopping time and motion, photography "emplit de force la vue,"[15] forcibly fills up our view. Photographs come to us like documents from "the other side," beyond time, beyond life. They are like testaments, last wills drawn up in the service of memory.

The power of photography, thus conceived, is intrinsic to the medium. It does not critically depend on artistry or aesthetics, on an inner vision in the mind of the photographer seeking expression. Iconic photographs, freezing history into memory, have an autonomy of expressive force unconnected to authorial intent or control. Even that most anonymous, almost authorless, of genres—the passport picture—can at times produce iconic photographs. In his book *Reading American Photographs* Alan Trachtenberg devotes a chapter to "illustrious Americans."[16] He takes the reader back to the pre–Civil War era in American history, reconstructing for us the way that leading public figures, pillars of republicanism, had their portraits taken in studios, such as Mathew Brady's in New York, that doubled as portrait galleries open to the public. There on display were the solemn, self-important faces of a white male elite whose collective charge was the commonweal of the Republic. The display served as public affirmation of an established civic order. Then Trachtenberg shifts focus. He confronts us with a body of photographs taken for scientific purposes and documenting the physical features of America's slave population. Unlike the portraiture of ranking public figures, authorially constructed to reflect older, painterly conventions of representation, no such artistic intervention occurred in the photographs of Southern slaves. They were reduced to mere objects for scientific observation, de-individualized if not dehumanized. They sat naked, their human dignity taken away, exposed to the cold, mechanical eye of the camera. Yet, as they look us in the face across a span of almost a century and a half, in spite of the humiliation and dehumanization the sitters refuse to be turned into objects. There is resistance in their eyes, individual strength, the fire of human life. Irrespective of authorial intent, the photographs restore their human dignity and confront us, after all these years, with the indignity of slavery. While the photographs thus turn into iconic pictures of life under slavery, the sitters turn into illustrious Americans, as representative of human dignity and strength as the icons of civic rectitude in Brady's gallery. Of course, without Trachtenberg's creative intervention, helping us to read these photographs while suggesting a radically different, radically more inclusive reading of citizenship and republicanism, the photographs might have lingered in historical limbo. Yet he has not created something that was not there. He may have helped us listen, but the voice we hear is that of the photographs rather than his. Unadorned, stark, purely mechanical exposures—photographs like these testify to the innate power of the medium.

Even more closely resembling passport photographs are pictures taken of inmates of the Tuol Sleng prison in Phnom Penh in Cambodia between 1975 and 1979. Of more than fourteen thousand people sent to s-21, as this prison was known, all but seven were executed. The Khmer Rouge's blunt renaming of the prison, formerly a school, as "s-21" was unintentionally eloquent, reflecting the way in which those who passed through the school gates and were executed inside became mere numbers themselves. Their killers—self-styled enemies of bureaucracy—

turned out to be expert and meticulous bureaucrats themselves. Not only did they keep a written record of each prisoner, including copies of confessions, they also took a photograph of every one. Following the chaotic retreat of Pol Pot's forces, much of the archive was looted and destroyed. Later, the U.S.-based Photo Archive Group helped to salvage some six thousand negatives, which are housed at the former school, now a museum commemorating the holocaust inflicted on Cambodia. Although the name of the photographer is now known to us—he was a boy in his late teens when he became chief photographer at Tuol Sleng—the haunting quality of the images is due to no authorial intent. Of course, background knowledge helps us to position these photographs as so many individual documents of mass slaughter, of Cambodia's killing fields. Like the murderous machine that would kill them, the photographs are machine documents—cold, mechanical shots of people facing their death. They are tagged, reduced to numbers, on the conveyor belt to execution. Many photographs show traces of other nonhuman agency, adding to their symbolic value. One photograph, of inmate number 86, shows a young boy with his hands (tied?) on his back, looking us in the face, fearful and utterly vulnerable. Inklike blots stain the picture, partly covering the young man's forehead. They are suggestive of landmasses on the map of an alien world where such unspeakable horror took place. But more than anything they suggest the blood that he, like so many before him, is doomed to shed. Another photograph, of an anguished young woman, has erratic lines running down from the top, as if signs of the way her life would soon be torn to pieces.[17]

If these examples testify to the "savage silence" of photography and account for its power to produce iconic images in the absence of any authorial agency or intent, this is of course not the whole story. In the store of iconic photographs that we all carry in our minds, many do show the hand of their maker and will be forever connected to that maker's name. Thus Robert Capa's celebrated Spanish Civil War picture of a Republican soldier falling backward under the impact of a mortal bullet became an icon of that tragic war, while at the same time establishing Capa's fame as a photojournalist. The photograph, along with a similar one of a different soldier, was published in the French photomagazine *VU* in September 1936, but both the photograph and its author became internationally celebrated when *Life* magazine published it in July 1937. Despite research aimed at demonstrating that the photograph was staged, it has managed to preserve its iconic value, while Capa lived on as one of the great photojournalists of the twentieth century. He was killed in Indochina in 1954, covering another war.[18]

The reputations of many other photojournalists are critically linked to iconic photographs they produced. There is the case of Eddie Adams, which I mentioned before. Author of the famed picture "Viet Cong Executed," he was awarded the 1969 Pulitzer Prize while his picture was named best photo of the year in the World Press Photo Competition and would win four more major journalistic awards. At the height of the Tet Offensive it was the single image that dramatized for many what sort of war America was engaged in. This picture, along with other celebrated photographs of the atrocities of the war, such as Ron Haeberle's "My Lai Massacre" (published in *Life* on March 16, 1968), definitively delegitimized America's involvement in the war. As iconic photographs do, they took on a meaning far transcending the mere documenting of a specific incident. Such images come to represent and symbolize the larger features of a historic episode, condensed into a single picture. Usually, in the long afterlife of Adams's picture, we see a cropped version of his full photograph, singling out the mortal confrontation between the South Vietnamese police chief and the Vietcong prisoner. The full photograph, as reproduced in *World Without End*, widens the frame to take in a South Vietnamese soldier storming up on the left, with teeth bared, and a policeman to the right running into the frame with his head turned away.[19] He must have simply missed the moment and hadn't seen it coming. Even so, there is no hint of the presence of other media people, photographing or filming the event. This seems to confirm what iconic photojournalism suggests about its authors and the way they work. Their mythology projects them as lone hunters in heroic pursuit of Cartier-Bresson's "decisive moment," out there by themselves to bear witness for the entire world. And their professional community, self-servingly, tends to sustain the myth. "Edward T. Adams lives and breathes photography," the Associated Press publication, *The AP World*, stated after Adams won the Pulitzer Prize. "He is one of the most accomplished photographers alive, and he pursues opportunity relentlessly."[20] Yet there were other cameramen at work, capturing the same moment. There is film footage of the event that puts it back into its time frame, reducing the shooting

The napalm girl, Kim Phuc. Nick Ut, photographer. Full frame and version cropped by Ut. *Associated Press.*

to just a passing moment. It may be true that the rival footage takes away from the illusion of the lone witness; on the other hand it allows for a comparison of the two media. As I argued before, it adds to our awareness of the singular, iconic power of still photographs.

In the case of Nick Ut's celebrated photograph of the napalmed Vietnamese children, similar comparisons may be made between film and photography, leading to the same conclusion. Again, Ut's iconic photograph may have suggested his presence as a lone, and alert, witness. It is an illusion that he may have carefully nurtured himself. As it turns out, the iconic photograph that affected the worldwide reading of what the Vietnam War was all about was only one among several pictures he took. Ut kept shooting while the children came running toward him. The pictures he chose to keep for himself differ in a number of respects from the one he published. The iconic image shows soldiers in the background, a fitting complement to a war photograph. The others, though,

show people wielding cameras, busy like Ut to capture the moment. Those photographs in a sense show the conditions of their own making and take away from the illusion of unmediated confrontation with the horror of war. The iconic photograph suggests the absence of a maker; the others insert a mediating layer of reporters filling the space between observer and picture. If the final, iconic image derives its power from selection, if not manipulation, by the maker, it may teach us that in many cases the illusion of direct confrontation is a construct. Photography, as I argued, as a mere mechanical device is inherently able to produce iconic views of history, yet it may be helped along by creative artists in producing this effect.

Yet there is more to be learned from Ut's set of photographs. Comparing the unpublished ones to the one that caught the world's attention also makes us aware of the contributing role of aesthetics in producing the final impact of an image. Precisely such aesthetic considerations

The napalm girl, Kim Phuc. Nick Ut, photographer. Full frame and version cropped by Ut. *Corbis Inc.*

must have guided Ut's hand when cropping the full photograph to the image that he made public. The drama conveyed by Ut's iconic rendition is helped much by the way the frame is filled, by its balance between foreground and background, giving central position to the girl running toward the viewer. Her brother in the lower left-hand corner, with his lower legs already outside the frame, and two smaller running children to the right make for a diagonal reading that reinforces the centrality of the screaming girl. Whatever the other potent reasons Ut may have had for selecting this one picture, its aesthetics as a composition must have weighed heavily in the balance. This may strike some readers as disconcerting if not actually offensive—who cares about bourgeois aesthetics when the subject is human suffering?—yet if we wish to understand how images affect us the way they do, we cannot but take this aspect into consideration. As the illustrations printed in this chapter may show, in the case of the second unpublished photograph no amount of cropping

could have given it the power of the cropped edition of Ut's iconic picture.

Something else may be at play in the case of entirely different iconic images, such as Lewis Hine's classic image "The Madonna of Ellis Island" or Dorothea Lange's "Migrant Mother." Part of the explanation of their iconic status, of their capturing in one single image the phenomenon of mass immigration or the plight of people struggling to survive the Great Depression, is due to the fact that these images inscribe themselves into a larger, collectively remembered iconography of "Mother and Child," helped in Hine's case by the enigmatic smile on his Madonna's face, reminiscent of the *Mona Lisa.* Such images help viewers place them in established frameworks of interpretation and thus facilitate their own reading. It is precisely the visual intertextuality that adds to the resonance of individual images. Even in the case of quasi-mechanical, quasi-objective images of passport-like quality that I discussed above, there must be such intertextuality. Couldn't it be that when looking at such images there is a resonance with our own mirror image? Couldn't it be that, through such heartrending pictures of people looking death in the face, we see our own face shimmering as we look at it intently in the mirror? Isn't that what makes for the individual impact of such photographs, this submerged sense of looking ourselves in the face? "There but for fortune. . . ."

The afterlife of iconic photographs is most clearly the area where the photography of history blends into the history of photography. From this perspective photographs most clearly take their place as agents of history, rather than being its mere reflection. From the moment that photographs acquire iconic status and enter the realm of the mass circulation of images, they begin to affect history rather than merely reflecting it. If Eddie Adams's picture came to be referred to as a "shot" that rang around the world, this meant his image had begun to affect the course of history. Its reading was symbolically expanded into an image representing everything that was wrong with the Vietnam War and America's role in it. Public opinion was affected by this and other such images, tilting the balance against further involvement, whatever the balance of forces on the battlefield.[21] But there are longer lines to be traced in the history of iconic photographs. Much as they may turn individual human beings who are pictured in them into mere emblems, occasionally their objects reenter history as individual subjects precisely because of their emblematic status. Thus, continuing interest in the fate of Nick Ut's napalmed girl—whom he was the first to get to a hospital, seeing to it that she received proper treatment rather than being left to die—led to a full-scale documentary of her life, from postwar Vietnam to self-chosen exile in Canada. The documentary culminated in her appearance at a Veterans Day event at the Vietnam Veterans Memorial in Washington, D.C., where she offered forgiveness. Had she not been an iconic figure in the first place, but simply one of those forgotten thousands who suffered her fate but went unnoticed by international photographers, her reappearance as an individual person would never have been newsworthy. She, however, reentered history and again made front-page news.

There are many less dramatic, more ironic, instances of the recycling of iconic images. In the area of mass culture, there is the image of Marilyn Monroe on a subway grating, her skirt billowing up. It is an image popping up all over the place, most memorably perhaps in Quentin Tarantino's *Pulp Fiction,* a film that thrives on postmodern intertextuality. And of course there is Che Guevara's messianic image, caught by Cuban photographer Alberto Korda, living its decontextualized life as a T-shirt image. More often than not, iconic images are being recontextualized, in the service of causes far removed from their historic moment of origin. Memories of Holocaust photographs now inform our reading of contemporary atrocity scenes, whether or not on acceptable historical grounds. Our response in such cases is programmed by historical memories, remembered images. At times historic photographs pop up triggered by recent events, as in the case of Secretary of State Colin Powell's lame attempt at convincing the United Nations Security Council of Iraq's possession of weapons of mass destruction. It reminded many, who had a photographic memory, of Adlai Stevenson as the U.S. delegate to the Security Council, making a much more convincing case based on aerial photography of the Soviet missile buildup on Cuba. If photographs are not necessarily iconic from birth, they can become so by later reference.

In our postmodern times, in which the very idea of an authenticated reading of history has been shelved as an untenable hegemonic discourse, the afterlife of iconic photographs takes many unexpected turns. The iconic image of Jack Ruby shooting Lee Harvey Oswald has now appeared as "Oswald/Ruby as Rock Band," in a 1996 photo-montage by George E. Mahlberg. Ruby is shown playing a guitar, rather than holding a gun. Oswald's scream of pain is turned into the howl of a pop singer, with his hands holding a microphone to his mouth. The undercover police officer to the left is now playing a keyboard.[22] What to make of this? The point, I assume, is to reduce epochal events to the status of mere media events, all of equal import and totally interchangeable. The point may well be a critique of contemporary media culture, but I am not sure. Take the case of Eddie Adams's "Viet Cong Executed." It is being recycled in a 1991 photograph by Yasumasa Morimura titled "Slaughter Cabinet I." Part of the collection of the Art Gallery of New South Wales, it is a picture of an ornate television console, with its doors swung open at 135-degree angles to make diagonals taking the viewer's gaze toward the central television image, in gelatin-silver print, of a staged version of Adams's iconic image. There is a zebra crossing behind the lethal confrontation, absent in Adams's picture; the facades along the street are different; the individuals involved in the picture are different, dressed in businessmen's attire complete with cuff links; yet the similarity to Adams's picture is striking.[23] Again the question arises as to what we are to make of this. Is the point to reduce an iconic picture to just another interchangeable, and forgettable, television image? Is the staging, with its reference to an urban setting more familiar to Australian urbanites, meant to convey a message of "It could happen here"? Or is it just postmodern playfulness, out to upset our established conventions of making sense of history?

The Iconic Photograph That Never Was (Nor Will Be?)

There is a rich visual record of the traumatic events of 9/11, the day that terror (and, as it later turned out, terrorists) struck the United States. The attack on the World Trade Center in New York is most richly documented. Tens of thousands of stunning photographs, which will forever reflect the images that burned themselves into our collective memory, show the many faces of the cataclysm. Many have become iconic through the epic concentration that their frames provide to what at the time may have seemed unfathomable. They now appear as catching the essence of the moment, the horror, the heroism, as well as the grim beauty of it all. Yet this was not a volcanic eruption, not a natural disaster. This is what men did to fellow human beings. They had set out indiscriminately to bring thousands to an untimely death.

Many sat in front of their television screens trying to imagine in anguish and impotence what was going on in the towering inferno of the World Trade Center. Yet one response among those trapped in the buildings above the level of impact was clear for all to see. Rather than burn or choke to death people by the hundreds were opting for a death of their own choosing, delivering themselves to the pull of gravity as they jumped from windows on all four sides of the towers. Television images showed many of these hapless individuals until the various channels covering the events stopped broadcasting them. The images were deemed too gruesome, too unmediated a confrontation with the horror of the moment. An additional consideration may have been that the images were seen as appealing to the voyeurism of the spectators, as too much of an unseemly intrusion into the utter loneliness of those who were only seconds away from death. Although the "jumpers" epitomized most starkly the horror and tragedy of the event, images of their free fall were safely tucked away from the public gaze, preventing their becoming part of a collective memory that would soon be cast in terms of the heroism and bravery of the victims and their saviors. Yet the mental shock and trauma of those who beheld the spectacle of so many people falling, and who will never forget the loud thud of bodies hitting the ground—"it was raining bodies," as one firefighter wailed in shock once he was safely back at his station[24]—does seem to need its own closure through sharing the memory with others.

What is it exactly about images of these lonesome people falling to their death that elicits public reticence? Is it the gulf between their experience, lasting not more than thirty seconds, and that of a larger public yearning to empathize yet prevented from empathy in the case of the falling people? Is it so hard to recognize a redeeming grandeur in their fate? Tellingly, one photograph related to this particular tragedy did make its way around the world and reached iconic status. One of the falling people hit a fireman on the ground and killed him. The fireman's body was anointed by Father Mychal Judge, whose own death, shortly thereafter in one of the two towers, was embraced as an example of martyrdom after the photograph—the redemptive tableau—of firefighters carrying his body from the rubble reached the public eye. Apparently Father Judge's display of compassion and humane grace in the hour of his own death made it easier to see redemptive value in the photograph, and to evoke the empathy of the many.

The rich store of photographs and of film and television footage may allow makers of historical documentaries to return to the images of falling people and carefully to contextualize them. Ric Burns, for example, in his documentary film *New York: The Center of the World*, has a section on 9/11.[25] He has chosen to give it the narrative structure of a biblical passion, telling a story that makes it clear to the viewer that the horror of the terrorist onslaught has made for the collective redemption of New Yorkers. Good in the end emerged from evil. Burns has not shrunk, for fear of being disrespectful to the dead, from showing footage of people leaning out of the upper floors of the two towers, clinging to windowpanes first, then choosing a free fall to certain death. The camera pans from body after body falling down to the stunned faces of the crowd. "My God, Oh, my God," is the continuing litany one hears. There is one voice, though, addressing the cameraman—one must assume—shouting: "You can't take pictures of this." That voice must have spoken on behalf of all those whose gut feeling was one of revulsion against filming this particular aspect of the horror of the World Trade Center attacks.

That feeling must have prevailed in the days following 9/11. The history of a photograph of one man falling, taken by Associated Press photographer Richard Drew, testifies to this urge to suppress. Drew had trained his telephoto lens on one man and shot eight frames. Back in his office at the Associated Press, he inserted the disc from his digital camera into his laptop and recognized, instantly, what only his camera had seen with its uncanny power to catch the optical unconscious. A moment no observer's eye could have consciously noticed was forever frozen in a frame. There was something iconic in the extended annihilation of a falling man. Drew did not even look at any of the other pictures in the sequence. He didn't have to. "You learn in photo editing to look for the frame," he says. "You have to recognize it. That picture just jumped off the screen because of its verticality and symmetry."[26] The next morning the photograph appeared on page 7 of the *New York Times* and in a number of other newspapers across the country. Yet, as Richard Drew remembers it, "Most newspapers refused to print it. Those who did, on the day after the World Trade Center attacks, received hundred of letters of complaint. The photograph was denounced as coldblooded, ghoulish and sadistic. Then it vanished."[27]

Drew had photographed dying before. As a twenty-one-year-old rookie photographer on a supposedly routine assignment, he was standing behind Robert F. Kennedy when he was assassinated. He was so close that Kennedy's blood spattered onto his jacket. He kept taking photographs even when a distressed Ethel Kennedy tried to fend off the intrusive camera eye. Nobody at the time refused to print those photographs. They became iconic images and established Drew's fame. What then is it about Drew's image of the falling man that people find so offensive?

As Tom Junod describes the photograph in his piece for *Esquire* magazine, it differs from all other photographs of people falling from the

Twin Towers. All the other images show people who appear to be struggling against horrific discrepancies of scale. They are made puny by the backdrop of the towers, which loom like colossi, and then by the event itself. They flail, twist, and turn; their shoes fly off. There is no semblance of control. The man in Drew's picture, by contrast, is perfectly vertical, head down, seemingly poised and in full control of his posture. The image shows him in perfect accord with the lines of the buildings behind him. He splits them, bisects them. Everything to the left of him in the picture is the North Tower; everything to the right, the South Tower. Junod goes on to say, movingly and perceptively: "Though oblivious to the geometric balance he has achieved, he is the essential element in the creation of a new flag, a banner composed entirely of steel bars shining in the sun. Some people who look at the picture see stoicism, willpower, a portrait of resignation; others see something else—something discordant and therefore terrible: freedom."[28] He does not appear intimidated by gravity's lethal force but rather seems to defy it. His arms are by his side. His left leg is bent at the knee, almost casually. He offers the ultimate image of grace in the face of death. Yet only seconds before or after, like the others who had jumped, he had flailed, twisted, and turned. No human eye could have caught this passing moment of transcendence.

To those who are willing to set aside their sense of disrespectful intrusion, this detached reading of the photograph suggests all the elements that make for an iconic photograph. In its suggestion of grandeur and grace, in its intertextual evocation of Jasper Johns's many variations on the theme of the American flag, it would appear to offer, in epic concentration, all that brought out the best in Man in the face of Man-made cataclysm. It would seem to make it the perfect American icon for the resilience of Americans at a time of national sorrow.

There may come a time when Drew's picture will be seen and remembered in its full iconic power, finding its place in the continued quest for the meaning of 9/11. Struggling to come up with the proper language, the proper metaphors, for understanding what the collapse of the Twin Towers may have signified, those reflecting on the meaning of Ground Zero may well come to construct their narratives around the central metaphor of the fall, in all its rich, intertextual resonance. In a perceptive essay, Devin Zuber, like Walter Benjamin's flaneur redivivus, reflects on the changed reading of one of the largest and most unknown public sculptures in lower Manhattan, several blocks north of the World Trade Center: Roy Shifrin's *Icarus*. The sculpture depicts Icarus at the very end of the Greek legend. The torso is headless and wingless, tilted at such an angle as to suggest not Icarus's winged ascension but his fall from the sky. The sculpture was positioned in such a way that the form was perfectly juxtaposed against the looming bulk of the Trade Center towers. At night one had the perspective of the statue falling down the dark space between the two towers. Only now can the sculpture assume its full mythological power as an emblem of human hubris "before the fall."[29] If the statue can be seen to prefigure 9/11, Art Spiegelman, in his *In the Shadow of No Towers*, after the fact creatively reconfigures the imagery and meaning of falling from the sky.[30] Once again using the medium of the comic book, or graphic novel, that he used so successfully before in *Maus*, Spiegelman tries to control the traumatic impact of witnessing the events of 9/11, and the flood of his earlier traumatic memories as a secondary Holocaust witness that 9/11 triggered in his mind. Plate 6 of *In the Shadow of No Towers* shows on the left-hand side a full-length image of one of the towers in the last moments before its collapse. A man is seen jumping from it, preferring the freedom of the sky above death by fire, performing, as the text has it, "a graceful Olympic dive as his last living act." The amazing thing is that the author admits that he is "haunted now by the images he didn't witness." What may have turned him into a secondary witness, much like the protagonist of *Maus*, may well have been Drew's image of what truly was a graceful Olympic dive captured by Drew's camera.[31]

FOUR ◉ FACES OF WAR

Mathew Brady, Stephen Crane, and the
Verisimilitude of Photography

BY 1851, WHEN American photographers Mathew Brady, Marin Lawrence, and John Whipple received the highest awards for their work at
London's Crystal Palace Exhibition, the power and prestige of this new
medium was clear. A decade later, President Abraham Lincoln confirmed the place of photography in American political culture when he
declared that a Brady portrait taken on the occasion of his speech at the
Cooper Union in New York City, and distributed nationally, had played
a major role in helping him win the presidency. In Washington at the
very outset of the Civil War it was again Mathew Brady, having just
photographed Lincoln's inauguration, who made *cartes de visite* for hundreds of departing soldiers, both fostering and satisfying a photographic
desire, a desire for the photograph, which, given the number of troops
in the city, can be understood, as Bill Brown points out, as a desire of the
masses.[1] Photography had sufficiently established itself in the public
mind as a new tool of memory—or mnemonic device—to satisfy the
need to keep absent loved ones pictorially present.

Yet it was the Civil War itself that would establish photography as a
medium affecting the way in which the general public would henceforth
be able to imagine such momentous historical events as war. Mathew
Brady and his team of war photographers for the first time in history

confronted audiences with images of the war as a machine producing corpses, thus radically changing their views of battlefields as fields of glory and heroism. His "Incidents of the War" exhibit in New York led the *New York Times* to award Brady "honorable recognition" for "mak-[ing] Photography the Clio of the war," proclaiming the exhibit to be "nearly as interesting as the war itself."[2] Alexander Gardner's photographs, displayed in the Brady exhibit, relentlessly foreground dead soldiers' faces and their mangled, strangely contorted bodies. The pictures fascinated the crowds in Brady's studio. And these spellbound crowds fascinated in turn contemporary writers, drawn by a longing to see viewers participate in a new ritual of morbid fixation. According to the *New York Times* account "groups [were] standing around these weird copies of carnage," or in Stephen Crane's words "bending down to look in the pale faces of the dead, chained by the strange spell that dwells in dead men's eyes." As the writer for the *Times* put it, the "terrible fascination" of the battlefield "draws one near these pictures, and makes him loath to leave them."

By the time that Stephen Crane re-evoked this morbid fascination in his 1895 novel *The Red Badge of Courage,* using the words just quoted, the impact of the Civil War photographs was already undergoing an ideological containment, as Alan Trachtenberg among others has argued.[3] The containment aimed at a nationalist memory of the Civil War as a testing ground. "The war as we see it now," John Ropes argued in 1891, was an "exhibition of the Anglo-Saxon race on trial," serving "to bring out [the] resolute and unyielding traits belonging to our race," its "unconquerable determination."[4] Yet, as Bill Brown argues, the act of reimagining the nation depended on "forgetting the photographic archive— or on remembering it, transforming it, within a different medium."[5] And that medium was the traditional wood engraving. In fact, at the time, photographic images could be mass produced only by rendering them as woodcuts. Popular as Civil War images were in the 1890s, what most people, including Stephen Crane, beheld were imitations of photographs, taking away photography's disturbing immediacy, while mediating its message. Photography is a mechanical art, yet it is capable— as Walter Benjamin, John Berger, Roland Barthes, and others remind us—of producing a *punctum,* an aura, an iconic force, that gets lost in translation to a different medium of mass reproduction, such as lithography or the wood engraving.[6]

Yet the disturbing fact remains that I could quote Crane alongside a *New York Times* account from 1862 *as if he had been there* to share the morbid fixation of the crowds in Brady's studio, "chained by the strange spell that dwells in dead men's eyes." I vividly remember from my first reading of Crane's Civil War novel how I dwelt on those passages where he evokes the fascination of staring dead men in the face. It brought back remembered pictures of death masks of deceased people lying in state and my sense of trespassing onto forbidden terrain. There may have been vaguely remembered mental pictures of dead family members, of a grandmother dying in my parents' house when I was still a child. Those mental pictures, photographs taken by our spellbound eyes—protophotographs, as it were, that may have readied the human mind for the invention and eager acceptance of photography—may account for the uncanny resemblance of Crane's writing and the war photographs of the Brady team. In what follows I explore this resemblance, conceiving of it as a parallel rather than a direct influence.

1. Parallels

This is an exploration of two parallels, two creative renderings of the Civil War, one photographic, the other literary. It is also a speculation on the virtual point where the two parallels meet—the point of perspectival intersection where the human gaze creates its own illusions. The first parallel, the photographic one, is a production fully contemporaneous with the Civil War. It consists of a corpus of visual images, instantly reflecting the face of war for those who were not there to witness the real event. War photographs had been taken before, but never on a scale as large as during the Civil War. One name in particular has become synonymous with this grand effort at photographic documentation: Mathew Brady's. At great personal expense, both financial and physical, he gathered a team of photographers and with them would cover the war from the first Battle of Bull Run through to the end. The second parallel is a work of literary imagination, by a man who had never yet seen war in his life: Stephen Crane's *The Red Badge of Courage*, written some thirty years after the war's end.

Given the obvious differences, in terms of time and medium, of documentation and imagination, how can the work of Brady and Crane be considered parallel? One answer is to look at the work from the angle of its reception by contemporaries. Not surprisingly, Brady's photographs of the war, and more particularly of the aftermath of bloody carnage, showing dead men stiffening in the chill air of morning, struck observers by their immediacy, their raw force that would forever alter the mode of visual representation of war.[7] The poignant pictures stunned Americans. Of Brady's photographs taken in the wake of the battle of Antietam, Oliver Wendell Holmes wrote in the *Atlantic Monthly:* "These terrible mementoes of one of the most sanguinary conflicts of the war, we owe to the enterprise of Mr. Brady of New York. We ourselves were upon the battlefield upon the Saturday following the Wednesday when the battle took place. The photographs bear witness to the accuracy of some of our sketches . . . the 'ditch' encumbered with the dead as we saw it . . . the Colonel's grey horse . . . just as we saw him lying . . . let him who wishes to know what war is, look at these series of illustrations."[8] Holmes knew of these details firsthand. The previous year he had rushed to the site of the Antietam battle in search of his wounded son, an experience he had recounted in the *Atlantic Monthly* in December 1862.[9] The Antietam pictures of the battlefield reminded him of that earlier experience. It was, he says in the 1863 article, "so nearly like visiting the battlefield to look over these views, that all the emotions excited by the actual sight of the stained and sordid scene, strewed with rags and wrecks, came back to us, and we buried them in the recesses of our cabinet as we would have buried the mutilated remains of the dead they too vividly repre-sented." Remarkably, in the *Atlantic* essay on his son, he had managed to keep at bay emotions that welled up at the sight of the photographs a year later.

More surprisingly, Crane's work of fiction on the Civil War could cause a similar sense of verisimilitude, of lifelikeness, among those read-ers who remembered the war as veterans. As Christopher Benfey re-minds us: "Crane's battle scenes were so convincingly chaotic that one confused veteran was moved to claim that he had been with Crane at Antietam."[10] Needless to say, Crane, born in 1871, had not been at An-tietam, unless in a previous incarnation.

The metaphor of a parallel between the work of Brady and Crane ap-plies at yet another level. If the alleged verisimilitude was part of the im-pact of their work at the point of reception, this was not simply a matter of a likeness as perceived by the audience. It was more likely the outcome of an effect, consciously contrived by the writer in emulation of the tools of the photographer. At a time, in the late nineteenth century, when writers had begun to ponder the problems of authorial mediation in their rendering of reality, photography provided them with the metaphors to outline the writing strategy of realism. Zola and other French realists had spoken of realism as a studied objectivity before the subject, a writing-as-if-one-were-not-there, which only the camera could describe. This view of photography as providing a "window" onto experience provided the French realists with the program for their writing. As Zola put it, the writer "ought to be the photographer of phenomena; his observations ought to represent nature exactly."[11] In America, Hawthorne's fictional character of Holgrave, the photographer in *The House of the Seven Gables,* had already given radical expression to this view of photography as an instrument to catch reality without human agency. "There is a wonderful insight in heaven's broad and simple sunshine. While we give it credit only for depicting the merest surface, it actually brings out the secret character with a truth that no painter would ever venture upon." Photography then, as the word implies, becomes purely the act of "writing with sunshine." In the new relationship between writing and seeing, here suggested, photography served as more than a mere metaphor. The new medium forced artists at the time to reconsider established modes of representation and to become more aware of acts of *seeing* as they relate to acts of writing, or painting, or other such means of artistic expression. Joseph Conrad's famous credo from the preface to *The Nigger of the Narcissus* turns this challenge into a writerly program: "All art . . . appeals primarily to the senses, and the artistic aim when expressing itself in written words must also make its appeal through the senses, if its high desire is to reach the secret spring of responsive emotions. . . . My task which I am trying to achieve is, by the power of the written word to make you hear, to make you feel—it is, before all, to make you *see.*"[12] The ultimate irony here, of course, is that if this program is radically pursued, a double vision on the part of the writer is the necessary outcome. An emphasis on seeing refers to the writer's inner eye, with which he explores the story world conjured up by his imagination; it may also lead him toward seeing himself engaged in the act of writing, as a subliminal awareness threatening to undermine the realist illusion of narration. It is an irony most fully brought to light by Michael Fried in his analysis of the way that the scene of writing may have metaphorically penetrated into Crane's prose, when, for instance, the picture of his hand forming letters on paper may have translated in the image of ants crawling across a dead man's face. Fried repeatedly stresses, though, that Crane can only have been (must have been) oblivious to his own fixation on the scene of writing as well as to his compulsive thematizing and foregrounding of writing.[13]

Whatever the case, Stephen Crane was sufficiently a child of his time to share in the language of neutrality. He and his friend Harold Frederic wrote appreciations of each other's work in terms of the truth or accuracy of recording. "Like the camera which exposed the romantic distortions of generations of battle painters, Crane's 'photographic revelations' suddenly illumined the authentic face of war," Frederic wrote of Crane. And Crane reciprocated by praising his friend's craftsmanship and comparing his mind to a "sensitive plate exposed to the sunlight of '61–'65."[14]

In the case of Crane's New York writings, as in his novel *Maggie: A Girl of the Streets*, an actual link with the documentary force of photography has been shown to exist. In all likelihood a first draft of the novel had been written before Crane arrived in New York. Rather than direct personal experience of city life, Jacob Riis's photographs of New York's slum dwellers, among other sources, had fired Crane's imagination.[15] How tempting, then, to assume that in the case of Crane's vivid representation of the Civil War the work of Brady and his associates played a similar role. For almost a generation after the Civil War the war photographs passed from public view. In the 1880s, however, interest revived, and a torrent of reproductions flooded the illustrated press. In 1888 *Battles and Leaders of the Civil War* was published in four volumes. The illustrations for these volumes were wood engravings made from negatives that had once belonged to Brady. According to Alan Trachtenberg, Crane himself credited these four volumes for helping in his descriptions of combat and soldiers.[16] If this is true—unfortunately, Trachtenberg does not substantiate his allegation, nor have I seen it confirmed by other sources—the fact remains that all that Crane would have seen were wood engravings rather than the war photographs themselves. As Trachtenberg himself makes clear in a reference to Brady's pre–Civil War daguerreotypes, reproduced as lithographs in the *Gallery of Illustrious Americans*, the lithographs are like a translation of the voice of the original daguerreotypes into the language of lithography. "In translation, Brady's daguerrean images lose their magical presence. The tales they tell are, as it were, in the voice of a ventriloquist. [The] . . . prints and [the accompanying] biographies impose on the original daguer-reotypes another notion of history—not the idea of the past magically returning to life, but an idea of the past as an ideological message."[17] On this ground, then, we cannot really argue that Crane's vivid visions of the Civil War have been meaningfully informed by a direct confrontation with the medium of photography, or that he was aware of the role that Brady had played in producing the corpus of photographic images of the war.

2. Parallels Intersecting?

Is there no way, then, in which we can move beyond the exploration of parallels, beyond the obvious statement that the work of Brady and affiliates and that of Crane are each in their own right a parallel to the Civil War, each of uncanny verisimilitude? Indeed, Crane's approach to writing may have taken its cue from the power of photography. But could we possibly go further and find a point where Brady's and Crane's renderings of the Civil War can be seen meaningfully to intersect? While avoiding Doctorow's kind of doctoring of history, where persons who never met in history are made to interact in the realm of fiction, I shall have occasion to show how tantalizingly close Crane and Brady came to meeting, like ships that passed in the night. But first let us look more closely at the central significance of Brady's and Crane's work on the Civil War.

Brady's Civil War photographs date from a time when cameras were still so cumbersome and exposure times so long as virtually to rule out the possibility of shooting action pictures. War in a sense had to come to a standstill for cameras to be able to capture it. Yet nothing need have kept Brady and his crew from presenting war in the traditional vein of gallantry, heroism, and romantic coloring. Clearly, though, this was not what he was after. Whether or not he asked people, from common soldiers to commanding officers, to pose for him, his pictures are always unadorned. The faces he shows are those of men who have seen battle or are getting ready for it. They are always of serious mien. They are posing, never posturing. They are staring death in the face. And when Brady shot soldiers who had already been shot, the only difference is that death stares *us* in the face. In war, a thin line divides the quick from the dead. Death rather than victory is the outcome of war. This was the message that Brady wanted to convey in his obsessive pursuit of the shifting lines of battle. And obsessive it was, as any selection of his battlefield pictures will make clear.

3. Intermezzo: A Subtext Emerges

In the previous few paragraphs a subtext to my argument has begun to push to the surface. It will do so again at the end of my exploration. As a submerged argument, it may have taken its cue from photography as a metaphor used over a century ago by those involved in the project of realism as an artistic aspiration. Once stirring, though, it refuses to move along nicely with my exploration of what I called the verisimilitude in the work of Crane and Brady. I had better acknowledge it now and weigh its implications for my use of the word verisimilitude. If, in the realist mode, photography was seen as "representing nature exactly," as a tool allowing optical realism, catching reality without human agency, what are we to make of this in our age of semiotic sophistication? We have become too much aware of the manipulative hand of the photographer, from the moment he chooses his angle through to the final compositional steps in the darkroom. Rather than providing a window onto reality, he sets a frame, constraining our view, directing our gaze. Yet, unmistakably, photographs derive their fascination from a quality inherent in the medium, regardless of the maker. They evoke an emotion that only rarely happens to us in real life, calling forth those moments where our individual minds act like photographic plates. We all know those moments that have etched themselves onto our minds like photographic stills: a farewell forever, a last glance at a beloved face, a sudden reunion, a sudden death. A camera does it all the time, casually catching fleeting moments that in the flux of real life we might never have noticed. Photographs, therefore, in addition to being referential, representing reality as the camera saw it, are always at the same time self-referential. Their intrinsic significance lies in their power to remind us of our own frail powers of observation and recollection. They are, therefore, in the way they affect us, surprisingly essentialist. They are able to convey the disturbing sense of witnessing reality as it really was, as no human eye could have caught it at the time. In that sense they are like objets trouvés, fossilized views, allowing us to ponder meanings that would otherwise have escaped us. Or, as Susan Sontag put it in a reference to Roland Barthes's interest in photography, "he treats [it] as a realm of pure haunted spectatorship. In [his] account of photography in *Camera Lucida* there are hardly any photographers—the subject is photographs (treated virtually as found objects) and those who are fascinated by them: as objects of erotic reverie, as *memento mori.*"[18] This is clearly the language of an era that has declared the death of the author. There are no more photographers, only photographs, or for that matter only texts. Ever since Roland Barthes's seminal exploration of the status of photographs as mediating between visible objects and the eyes of beholders, in ways characteristically distinct from any other way of representation, we can no longer share the naive realist views of a century ago. Yet, if we take Barthes's cue and look at photographs as objects of erotic reverie, as memento mori, there are those stunning cases of photographs as truly "objets trouvés," the products of chance rather than of human agency. There is the unforgettable glass plate of Lincoln, which was exhibited by Brady's gallery. Fate has left us with only this broken plate, as if in prescience of Lincoln's fate. There is another picture of Lincoln, also exhibited by Brady's gallery, on which a nonauthorial process of chemical decay has worked to produce a halo around the head of the sitter, equally affecting the way we now view the picture. Both pictures, in their serendipitous ways, might be taken ironically to illustrate the realist's view of old that saw photography as a way of representing reality without human agency. But the more general implications of Barthes's approach take us in a similar direction. If there is still human agency at work, it is no longer that of the photographer, but of the spectator. If photographs have meanings, the one meaning overriding all others is that of a memento mori, of a confrontation with time at a standstill, with moments that are gone forever. In that sense Brady's Civil War photographs, whatever his authorial manipulations, are self-reinforcing in their removal of the author from view. Brady's focus on war as a machine producing dead bodies enhances the impact of his pictures as so many reminders of our own mortality, our human condition.

Anthony Berger, photographer. Abraham Lincoln (1864). *O. Stendorf Collection, Library of Congress.*

T. P. Pearson, photographer. Abraham Lincoln (1858). *Mellon Collection.*

4. Same Question: Parallels Intersecting?

How about Crane? Not a photographer, how can he possibly be drawn into a comparison once we have set photographs apart as a medium sui generis? The question should then be one of the effect of writing as compared to that of photographic images. Could it be that at the point of reception, by a reader or a spectator, a similar sense is produced of unmediated confrontation with reality, etching itself onto our minds with quasi-unmediated force? Crane's Civil War novel can of course be read in a number of ways. A common view sees it as a novel of initiation, of a boy becoming a man. This is the common view in literary textbooks, introducing high school students to the literary canon. Another view would be to judge the novel according to some naive standard of the realistic portrayal of war. One way in which the book certainly cannot be read is as a specific portrayal of the Civil War in terms of its causes. As Daniel Aaron has remarked, "Negroes and Lincoln and hospitals and prisons are not to be found in Crane's theatre."[19] Recently, a different reading of the book has been proposed by Christopher Benfey. As he argues, *The Red Badge of Courage* is indeed about an initiation, though not necessarily into manhood. I quote: "What Crane tried to imagine in *The Red Badge,* and what repeatedly captured his attention when he came to experience real war, was the fate of the body in human conflict. To put it another way, Crane found no better place than war to show the alarming fact—alarming to him and to his hero Henry Fleming—that human beings have bodies, and are therefore mortal."[20] *The Red Badge of Courage,* according to Benfey, can be read as a series of confrontations, of increasing intensity, with human corporeality. Crane orchestrates Fleming's progress in and out of battle as an education in wounds and corpses. The first view of a corpse is a critical moment, and Crane lingers over it:

Once the line encountered the body of a dead soldier. He lay upon his back staring at the sky. He was dressed in an awkward suit of yellowish brown. The youth could see that the soles of his shoes had been worn to the thinness of writing paper, and from a great rent in one the dead foot projected piteously. And it was as if fate had betrayed the soldier. In death it exposed to his enemies that poverty which in life he had perhaps concealed from his friends. . . . The youth looked keenly at the ashen face. The wind raised the tawny beard. It moved as if a hand were stroking it. He vaguely desired to walk around and around the body and stare; the impulse of the living to try and read in dead eyes the answer to the Question.

As Henry continues to wrestle with his problem, he encounters a series of wounded men, as though to find out by what processes men are turned into corpses. In one of the most celebrated and uncanny scenes of the novel, Henry stumbles through the woods until he reaches "a place where the high, arching boughs made a chapel." What follows is a sort of sacred rite, an initiation into the mysteries of life and death.

He softly pushed the green doors aside and entered. Pine needles were a gentle brown carpet. There was a religious half light. Near the threshold he stopped, horror-stricken at the sight of a thing. He was being looked at by a dead man who was seated with his back against a columnlike tree. The corpse was dressed in a uniform that once had been blue, but was now faded to a melancholy shade of green. The eyes, staring at the youth, had changed to the dull hue to be seen on the side of a dead fish. The mouth was open. Its red had changed to an appalling yellow. Over the gray skin of the face ran little ants. One was trundling some sort of a bundle upon the upper lip.

Each detail—the faded, green uniform, the dull hue of the eyes, the busy ants—draws this corpse back into the natural landscape, as if to prove that the body returns to dust.

The youth gave a shriek as he confronted the thing. He was for moments turned to stone before it. He remained staring into the liquid-looking eyes. The dead man and the living man exchanged a long look. Then the youth cautiously put one hand behind him and brought it against a tree. Leaning upon this he retreated, step by step, with his face still toward the thing. He feared that if he turned his back the body might spring up and stealthily pursue him.

As Benfey puts it: "The real lesson to be learned in this chapel is not the lesson of courage but the lesson of corporeality—and thence mortality."[21] There are many more scenes, of bodies wounded, of bodies in agony, to confirm this view. As is so often the case in Crane's work, he had imagined reality before experiencing it. And often his hunches proved strangely prescient. Thus, in *The Red Badge*, before his later experience of real battle, he came upon this crucial metaphor:

The battle was like the grinding of an immense and terrible machine to him. Its complexities and powers, its grim processes, fascinated him. He must go close and see it produce corpses.

Crane had no doubt about the real product of war. Several years later, in his journalistic reports from the battlefields in Greece, there is the gripping portrait of a wounded soldier, bloodied and bandaged, shot in the head, walking away from the battlefield.

Behind him was the noise of battle: the roar and rumble of an enormous factory. This was the product. This was the product, not so well finished as some, but sufficient to express the plan of the machine. This wounded soldier explained the distinct roar. He defined it.

One cannot avoid pausing at the bitter pun on "finished," at the confident use of repetition—"This was the product. This was the product . . ." —expressing both the repeated functions of the machinery and the pathos of the spectator's shocked response.

Here, I would argue, we hit upon the point where the work of Brady and Crane do intersect—the point where both "authors" produce texts, or render pictures, that turn our eyes into camera lenses, producing vivid pictures that leave a lasting imprint on our minds. They share a similar, disenchanted view of war as a machinery producing corpses. Brady could not stop recording this continuing process. Crane had imagined it before he went out to see his views confirmed in real battle. Given this affinity of views, between two kindred spirits, how could it be that the younger of these two sensitive minds had not been influenced by the obsessions of the older?

They came so tantalizingly close to the point where their lives might have intersected. When Crane was writing his Civil War novel, Brady, ailing, almost completely blind, bedridden, was planning an exhibit in New York of his war photographs. It was not to be. He died in December 1896, before his plans had come to fruition. He and his nephew by marriage, Levin Handy, had been active until Brady's end. They kept two studios going, one in New York, one in Washington, D.C. Crane had his photograph taken at a studio in New York whose branch in Washington was only a few blocks away from the Brady studio. In the Brady studio, in these late years, a group portrait was made of Mark Twain, flanked by two famous war reporters of the time, Ned House and George Alfred Townsend. Crane might have gone to Brady's studio. He didn't. Brady might have included Crane as a famous war correspondent. He didn't either. Their lives never met. Their works did.

5. The Subtext Resurfaces

If anything, authors have been at the center of our attention in the fore-going paragraphs. How does that affect our discussion of the verisimil-itude of their works, of the lifelike—or rather deathlike—quality of their views of war? Photographs and literary texts can be regarded as having meanings at the point of their reception, irrespective of authorial intent and strategy. They can on occasion convey a sense of immediacy, as if, beyond the text, beyond the picture, we are confronting reality directly. Yet this sense of verisimilitude, of catching the essence of an event con-densed in one iconic rendering, is never solely a matter of the reader's or spectator's imagination and sensibility. Serendipity apart, as in the case of the two Lincoln photographs where gravity and chemistry worked their effect, I would argue in conclusion that there is always the hand of a maker intervening. Our sense of verisimilitude is, more often than not, an effect intended by an author. Our sense of immediacy is not a matter of the audience excluding the author, eradicating him or her from view; it is often literally a matter of the author creating this effect. In the case of Crane, there is of course a long line of textual analysis outlining the writerly ways in which Crane manages to "make us *see*," which, when taken to its ironic extreme, as in the case of Fried's reading of Crane, makes us *see* Crane's authorial hand metaphorically transposed into the narrative. In the case of Brady's work as well, careful research has pointed up the moments at which corpses may have been moved from place to place or soldiers played dead for the camera. The staging of scenes, even scenes of death, suggests the photographer's desire to satisfy a need (his own or his audience's) for order, even that of theatricality.[22]

As a final sobering illustration I invite the reader to look again at two photographs from a later war in American history: the Vietnam War, the photographs by Nick Ut that I discussed earlier. The first photo-graph has become a part of our memory of the Vietnam War, an icon condensing the horrors of that war into one image. Its force is the force of essentialism: this is what the war really looked like, this is why we ab-horred it and went out into the streets in protest against it. Why then the sense of having been manipulated, even of having been "had," once we see this photograph alongside others that the photographer decided to leave unpublished? Particularly in the case of Ut's second photo-graph, reproduced in the previous chapter, the impression of direct confrontation vanishes. We become aware of mediating agents. We are in their hands. As if by a postmodern sleight of hand, we are being distanced, if not put in our place. We are made aware of the fact that this is a case of photographers doing their work, as in so many other places of distress and human suffering. More than that, we are made aware of the voyeuristic element in our interest, a voyeurism we now realize with shame we share with the crowd of photographers.

By publishing only the one photograph that we all remember, by keeping the other photographs stored and removing his colleagues from the scene, the photographer in a sense vanishes from the picture, creating the illusion that we were present on the spot ourselves. Ut was absolutely right, of course. Only in this way could he show us the horrible face of the Vietnam War. The picture could turn into an icon of reality only because the photographer chose to arrange reality for us.

FIVE ◉ COLD WAR PHOTOGRAPHY

Putting the Best Face on It

THE PREVIOUS CHAPTER left us studying a poignant picture. While it took us from the Civil War to another hot war in American history, the Vietnam War, the point was not chronology. When the issue is the power of iconic images, of iconic images of war in our case, we can freely range across time. Whether it was the Civil War or the Vietnam War, both produced images that leap out from the page, that come at us, and hit us, like arrows. This is what Roland Barthes had in mind when he spoke of the *punctum* of photographs, literally their poignancy. Yet, as he reminds us at the same time, a photograph's poignancy then leads to its *studium* when, following its impact, it holds our attention and forces us to look at it closely.[1] That is the moment when we begin to understand why photographers choose to publish one photograph from among a series shot at the same time, and to keep the rest under wraps. That is when we begin to study and understand what accounts for the power of iconic photographs. Aesthetic considerations do weigh in, as we saw looking at two of Nick Ut's shots of the napalmed girl. But we may ask ourselves whether in the end it is not the horror of war, of death and human suffering, that gives these photographs their poignancy and iconic force. In the absence of such drama, can photographs ever have comparable impact? Compared with photographic renderings of the hot spots of history, has the Cold War spawned a similar repertoire of images, of similar force? Do we remember the Cold War other than by photographs of its hot spots, the eruptions, the volcanic moments, whereas truly the Cold War is precisely the metaphor for the unspectacular, the nonseismic intervals of slow motion? Can there be iconic photographs of the Cold War? And if so, what are they like? What agency was involved in their creation and dissemination? Questions like these will guide our search in this chapter.

As one of the two main parties in a global struggle that we know as the Cold War, the United States had a vital interest in the ways it was perceived, at home and abroad, by friend and foe. Many were the eyes focused on America, in sympathy and affiliation or in a readiness to reject. Photography, by then, had come fully into its own as a medium of mass communication. It had given rise to a mass circulation of images that no single agent could any longer hope to control. Not the Soviet bloc, in spite of its alleged totalitarianism, not the vaunted "Free World" either, priding itself on its democracy and the pluralism of opinions and viewpoints. Yet opinions and viewpoints never exist in an ideological vacuum, entirely filling up the conceptual space of thinkable things. There is always the gravitational pull of a cultural mainstream, of a hegemonic reading of collective identity. When we revisit the photographic representation of America, particularly in the 1950s, we cannot but be struck by the consistency of the overall image, as belated testimony to the climate of consensus that allegedly held sway during that decade. If there is a controlling agency here, it is not that of party or state, as in the Soviet case. Yet it is ideological, in the sense of a collective outlook on life. It was shared by most rather than imposed from above; its agents were many, yet they worked in collusion—the world of business, the entertainment industry, advertisements, government agencies—and it was bought (so to speak) by a majority of what Lizabeth Cohen has felicitously called the "consumers' republic."[2] Much as she sets out to deconstruct the dream by looking at the realities behind it, she does not deny that the consumers' republic offered the joys of affluence to many, and tempted others with its promise. The camera eye may have been ubiquitous, yet the public eye beheld a body of photographs showing an American collective sense of the Good Life, centering on the family, the home, and the joys of consumption. *Life* magazine, in its innovative photo essays as much as in the advertisements that it carried, presented its middle-class readers with a collective picture in which they happily recognized themselves. Through its Atlantic edition, it allowed Europeans to look in from the outside, and many happily obliged. What was self-affirmation for Americans offered a panorama of the Good Life that Europeans saw beckoning on their Western horizon.

If this was the whole story, the American government, in its confrontation with world communism, could have simply sat back and relaxed. It chose not to. It saw enemies everywhere, not only abroad, but more surprisingly at home (under the bed) as well. What in hindsight remains truly amazing about the American obsession with a domestic communist fifth column is the fact that the lure of communism in the United States was so feeble. Registered members of the Communist party were a tiny handful; anticommunism, according to public opinion surveys from the 1930s through the 1980s, was firmly entrenched.[3] America's fears of radical ideas, seen as alien or un-American, have a long tradition. They have always been triggered by successful revolutions, in France in the late eighteenth century or in Russia in the early twentieth century, setting up ideological systems to rival the American creed in its universalism and views of mankind's future. Political scientist Louis Hartz once hypothesized that Americans were so ideologically straitjacketed that a philosophy not espousing individualism, equality of opportunity, and freedom would be seen as alien.[4] Anticommunism is only one variety of this larger allergy to rival, and more radical, readings of the course of history. In 1949, Arthur M. Schlesinger, Jr., wrote of the Cold War: "In its essence this crisis is internal."[5] Although he believed that the external communist threat was real, he felt that its real danger was the fear it engendered in the minds of most Americans. It gave rise to a politics of fear in what British poet W. H. Auden labeled "the age of anxiety." One United States president, Jimmy Carter, at one point referred to what he saw as "the inordinate fear of Communism." Other public figures, though, chose to bank on this fear, using it as a tool to further their own political ends. President Ronald Reagan, Carter's successor, revived the Manichaeism of America confronting the Soviet Union as "the evil empire." But Schlesinger's intimation of the real danger of the fear of communism had been proved right much earlier, in the early years of the Cold War. Then, in a veritable reign of terror, fear, and intimidation, the McCarthyite attempts at exorcising the evil spirit of communism threatened to turn the United States into the mirror image of the foreign foe it had set out to confront. In its foreign policy, the same logic was at work. If the Soviet Union had chosen to revive its prewar international Agitprop network of the Komintern, under the new name of the Kominform, America developed its own informal, undercover propaganda offensive. It was sponsored and funded by the CIA, outside democratic control, with a view to rallying the international democratic left to its anticommunist cause. As Frances Saunders convincingly argues, this illicit international propaganda strategy may have been well chosen. Given America's domestic clampdown on its left-leaning intelligentsia, Congress might well have looked unfavorably on attempts to court precisely such an intelligentsia abroad, using taxpayers' money.[6] Whatever the justification, though, the means toward the end again were the perfect mirror image of the enemy's means of combat. This, of course, is not an unusual story. One of the fathers of twentieth-century sociology, Georg Simmel, had already posited that parties locked in all-out combat will increasingly resemble each other in their choice of means, whatever the alleged difference in purpose. It is a useful reminder even today, when the United States, claiming to bring democracy to the world in its battle against international terrorism, rides roughshod over the civil and human rights protections central to its national and international commitments.

Locked in Cold War combat, then, on a path of its own choosing, the United States could not simply rely on the free flow of ideas and images to further its cause. Nor, on the other hand, did it need to entirely renounce such a flow. There was simply too much in its free-market production of mass culture that served its ends of presenting an enticing view of the country and its culture. As many cultural affairs posts reported back to Washington, there was a marked demand (if not a market) abroad for the full range of America's cultural production, from Hollywood films, cartoons, popular music, and writing to the very consumption goods that foreign audiences had watched Americans enjoy. If a doctrine emerged in this area of cultural diplomacy, it might be flippantly called the Marilyn Monroe doctrine.[7] If anything, the United States attempted to further this flow of its mass culture abroad by leaning on countries receiving Marshall Plan aid to open their markets, particularly for Hollywood films, and use some of their so-called counterpart funds to pay for them rather than plead insolvency.[8] There may have been dissenting views within the State Department, and more generally the foreign policy establishment, that would have promoted America's highbrow rather than its mass culture, yet the greater curiosity and demand abroad undeniably was for the latter. To the extent that highbrow art did get sent abroad under government auspices—American literature to United States Information Agency (USIA) reading rooms in Europe, for instance, or avant-garde painting to European museums of modern art—it ironically tended to run afoul of the middlebrow, philistine, and anticommunist watchdogs in Congress. Joseph McCarthy's cronies, the "dreadful duo" of Roy Cohn and David Schine, undertook a tour of USIA libraries in seven countries. They announced that thirty thousand books of the two million on the shelves were by "pro-Communist" writers and demanded their removal. As Frances Saunders tells the story, "[t]he State Department, far from defending its libraries (which were visited by 36 million people annually) issues a craven directive prohibiting any material, including paintings, by 'any controversial persons, Communists, fellow-travellers, et cetera.'"[9] In painting, America's Abstract Expressionist artists found themselves caught in the same cross fire. In Congress a Republican from Missouri, George Dondero, declared modernism to be quite simply part of a worldwide conspiracy to weaken American resolve. "All modern art is communistic," he declared. Where Dondero saw in Abstract Expressionism evidence of a communist conspiracy, America's cultural mandarins detected a contrary virtue: for them it spoke to a specifically American, and anticommunist, ideology, the ideology of freedom, of free enterprise. The philistines scored an early victory in 1947 when they forced the withdrawal of a State Department exhibition called "Advancing American Art," a selection of seventy-nine "progressive" works. The show had reached Paris, then moved on to Prague, where it was such a success that the Russians immediately sent in a rival exhibition. Far from advancing the cause of American art, though, the show signaled its ignominious retreat. In Congress it was denounced as subversive and "un-American." The show was canceled, and the paintings were sold off at a 95 percent discount as surplus government property. As in so many other areas, the CIA stepped in and turned to the private sector, including museums and collections of art, to promote American avant-garde painting abroad. Here again was that sublime paradox of American strategy in the cultural Cold War: in order to promote an acceptance of art produced in (and vaunted as the expression of) democracy, the democratic process itself had to be circumvented.[10]

Yet mainstream American culture, in its worldwide dissemination, was relatively safe from philistine scrutiny. In its general convergence with a consensual reading of America, it projected a view of America abroad much like *Life* magazine's. It also testified, or could at least be presented as doing so, to the vigor and vitality of America's free market for cultural production. Both elements blended beautifully to turn the package into a continuing advertisement for the American Way of Life. This mass-marketed culture was the ideal, and uncontested, tool for American cultural diplomacy. If, in addition to its other qualities, it could also serve in the battle over minds and hearts in the Cold War confrontation with the Soviet Union, this raises an interesting question. Does it mean that, looking back from our present vantage point, we can recognize the face of the Cold War in any of these cultural productions? As with all exploration of meaning, much of course depends on context, on the uses made of cultural products. Meaning resides in use. With this proviso in mind, let us proceed to an exploration of what the photographic face of the Cold War may have been.

The Face of the Cold War

Given the vast stores of information available on the World Wide Web and the power of our contemporary search engines, it is an interesting experiment to type in three words, Cold War photography, and to see what the results are. In terms of numbers, there are thousands of finds. They range widely. Many are relevant, for example references to books on the subject. Others are surprising, and confront us with the question raised above. Let me give just one example.[11] One item found was "Picturing Levittown: Gottscho-Schleisner's Architectural and Commercial Photographs of Levittown, Long Island, 1947–1958," by Peter B. Hales. The article is about the architectural photography firm of Gottscho-Schleisner, which worked along the East Coast of the United States from the mid-1930s through the late 1950s. Its pictures adorned the brochures and portfolios of architects and interior designers and appeared, usually without noticeable credit, in home improvement and decorating magazines like *House Beautiful*. Gottscho and Schleisner started working in

Levittown probably at the behest of the architect Morris Lapidus, whose firm was designing commercial structures in the new community. The article comes with illustrations, pictures of privately owned homes and stores. The photographs of the latter commercial structures are all from the early years, around 1950. But the photographers returned in the later 1950s to photograph some of Levittown's houses for the upscale magazine *House Beautiful*. According to Hales, "Now Levittown had grown up, the trees shaded wide streets, and the houses and lawns, gardens and yards had all taken on the character of their owner-occupants."[12] This may strike contemporary viewers, urbanites in particular, as overly generous in its empathy with the local residents. He is describing, after all, suburban America as it emerged in the postwar years, hardening the lines of class and racial segregation rather than producing the vaunted classless society of America's era of affluence. Suburbs like this were the islands of class and racial homogeneity, as so many outcomes of free-market mechanisms and political abstinence. They were also the stifling havens that younger generations rose up against in cultural rebellion in the 1960s. As such they already evoked an America seeking refuge in an age of anxiety. As such they may also, nowadays, turn these pictures into icons of Cold War America. Yet these are not the signals that triggered Google into bringing this piece to my attention. It is Hales's text accompanying photographs of Levittown's stores that provides the key words. As he phrases it: "One of the strengths of these pictures for us, now, 50 years later, is the way they articulate the postwar modernist look. In Lapidus' Holly Store children's section, the smaller display tables float on their tubular chrome legs, and the lighting fixtures give linear order to the scene. Gottscho-Schleisner used short focal-length lenses, wide-angle lenses, on view cameras—probably a $8\frac{1}{4}$ lens on a 4×5 Deardorff or the equivalents. This combination gave the swooping, exaggerated quality of the space, and made objects seem to rise off the floor, defying gravity." Interesting, all this, although it hardly redeems what we may now experience as a rather alienating setting. The following passage, though, is what triggered my search machine. "*Power* in all its implications, [*sic*] was at the center of the American Cold War experience. On one extreme were the global questions of America as a world power, and the powers of the Russian adversary, on the other, the more mundane but seductive promises of mechanical and technological power promised with the scientific-technical-manufacturing revolutions born in World War II and brought to fruition in the decade after the end of the war—big cars, cheap electricity, new appliances promising ease and comfort." Commenting on another photograph, of a Long Island Lighting Company appliance store, Hales argues that "all of that [i.e., the things he just mentioned] is present, and hidden at the same time. The picture was made in 1953, years before Richard Nixon would stand in a model kitchen at a trade exposition [in Moscow] and lecture Russian Premier Krushev about American ascendence on the wings of appliances, in the infamous 'kitchen debates.' But the ambience of the '50s came in part out of that sense that material prosperity, power, and global influence were all somehow, confusingly, linked together."

I will return to the kitchen debate later. The interesting point here is the way Hales, like so many other Americans at the time and later, connects the American Way of Life during the 1950s to the Cold War context. At the time of the Moscow kitchen debate the Soviet Union had just put the first Sputnik into space, yet Nixon—at least there and then, before the world press—managed to change the scorecard of the Cold War confrontation. From a space race he took it down to the level of a race between two rival economies, measured by their capacities to satisfy consumer demands. Khrushchev adopted the terms of their exchange and boasted that before long the Soviet Union would bury the United States under the Soviet plethora of consumer goods. It was dramatic testimony in support of Daniel Bell's intimation at the time that the end of ideology had set in. It may have seemed, briefly, as if the Cold War contest would henceforth proceed on American terms, with America turned into the moving target for others to aim at.

This may reflect an awareness that many Americans shared in their everyday lives. Their pride in owning their own homes, the satisfaction they felt when buying a new appliance, or a new car, may have been enhanced by this comparative measure of the superiority of the American Way. It is good to know you are number one in the world and to be able to read confirmation in every single act of purchase and consumption, in every advertisement that catches your eye, in every magazine you open. So if, as I argued before, the meaning of phrases such as Cold War culture is in their use, much of American postwar culture may meaningfully appear to us in its Cold War connection and be explored as such. Much of it, but therefore not all of it. Where to draw the line?

A number of American historians have recently been tackling this question. Alan Brinkley reduces the question to how it could have come about that so many Americans in the 1950s, critics of American culture included, shared a view of American culture and society as reflecting an essential unity of interests and values widely shared by Americans of all classes, regions, races, and creeds. "How was it possible for so many Americans to believe in something that now seems so clearly untrue? How did this illusion of unity become so important a part of American culture during the Cold War?"[13] Many observers, Brinkley argues, have given much of the credit to the Cold War itself, to the political repression that accompanied the rivalry with the Soviet Union, to the pressures that rivalry created to celebrate American society and affirm its right to leadership of the "Free World." He refers to Archibald Mac-Leish, who wrote as early as 1949: "Never in the history of the world was one people as completely dominated, intellectually and morally, by another as the people of the United States were by the people of Russia in the four years from 1946 to 1949." But Brinkley goes on to argue that other social and cultural transformations had at least as much to do with the shaping of what we now call "Cold War culture" as did the Cold War itself. As he puts it in concluding his argument: "American society and culture would likely have looked much the same in the 1940s and 1950s with or without the Cold War." Yet, formulated this way, the conclusion skirts the question of whether American culture in the 1940s and 1950s, in the absence of the Cold War, not might have *looked* the same, but *felt* the same. The experience and memories of those who lived through the period is as much a historical fact to be taken into account, illusory as it may have been. Peter Kuznick and James Gilbert, editors of the volume that contains Brinkley's piece, take a somewhat different approach to the tangled web of Cold War culture. They grant that the Cold War shaped and distorted "virtually every aspect of American life," yet broadly speaking they see very little fundamentally new about American culture in the Cold War era. "Much of the characteristics by which we define it are the results of long-term trends and political habits of mind, revived and refurbished from the past." Following a survey of long-term secular trends, of demography, of an expanding state role in society, of religion, of economic growth and suburbanization, of the role of the media, seen in interaction with novel developments connected with the new military threats and involvements on the world stage, the authors conclude: "We take strong issue with those observers who have found the

Cold War to be responsible for every change and cultural distortion occurring during these years. Nevertheless, the vividness of the perceptions suggests that the principal effect of the Cold War may have been psychological."[14] This conclusion does not take us much further in filtering out the specific Cold War element in America's Cold War culture.

Perhaps the question should be cast in less general terms, and be re-engaged in a more direct confrontation with the stubborn and resistant stuff that history leaves in its wake. Alan Trachtenberg did that when he wrote an introduction to the catalog of an exhibition—*The Tumultuous Fifties*—showing photographs from the New York Times Photo Archives, known as "the morgue."[15] Hundreds of photographs laid to rest there, deemed no longer newsworthy, were exposed to the public eye once again. "How to bring discarded filed-away newspaper images back to life as history is the challenge posed by this exhibition," Trachtenberg writes. Their main impact, as spectral images reappearing from a past we might have thought we had ordered and filed away, is to disturb such ideas of mastery of the past. "Once thought safely embalmed in historical memory as a time of shabby conformity, a drab background for nostalgia-inducing, machine-tooled furniture and the flamboyance of Elvis Presley, the fifties come to life in these photographic traces and show that these years can still trouble with their tumult and turmoil." Confronted once again, like the newspaper-reading public in the 1950s, with the multifaceted representation of everyday life and concerns, there is too great a variety to allow any overarching reading, any organizing metaphor. The Cold War is a clear presence in many of these pictures, yet, as Trachtenberg has it: "actual preoccupations lay elsewhere." That may be true, yet we should not forget that many of the shots we see here (of, e.g., clashes in the struggle for desegregation in the South) were shots seen around the world. They were published elsewhere and affected foreign audiences' views of the United States, west and east of the Iron Curtain. As such they became foreign policy concerns of the United States and began to function in Cold War propaganda battles. If meaning resides in use, such disturbing photographs do more than upset any homogenizing views of America's 1950s culture; they acquire a Cold War reading and may well serve to show us one more photographic face of the Cold War.

The Cold War, then, has many faces. The responses one obtains from simply and informally asking friends, relatives, students, and colleagues what photographic image comes to mind as the single most representative expression of the Cold War confirm this. Depending on a respondent's age and time range of memory, a typical Cold War picture may date from anywhere between the 1950s through the early 1990s. People may recall the Cold War in United States pictures or in European photographs. The context may be a shared us-versus-them perspective, of the West versus the East, or it may have to do with protest and resistance within the West, as in anti–Vietnam War demonstrations, in the United States and Europe, or anti–cruise missile marches in Europe. Anti-Americanism as much as Americanophilia make up this general frame of remembrance. Hot spots, moments when the Cold War heated up, as in the Korean War, the erection of the Berlin Wall, the Hungarian uprising, may be more likely to come up, though, than the cooler moments. Most people of a certain age have fond memories of American popular culture, in its many varieties, but they tend to store those in a separate memory file. Even those who had been the most radical anti-American protesters showed this compartmentalization in their views of American culture and American policies. Carrying banners calling Lyndon Johnson a murderer, they had dressed in blue jeans and T-shirts, had worn sneakers, and affiliated with the heroes of the American counterculture of the 1960s, if not with Elvis Presley and American popular culture more generally. When these protests appropriated American cultural forms, for their own private purposes, those forms never assumed the tinge of Cold War culture. Behind the Iron Curtain things may have been different. Wearing blue jeans was a form of political protest. Such regalia of Western culture did assume Cold War meanings that they lacked in the West.

In our explorations of the photographic faces of the Cold War we must keep an open eye for their context, for settings of reception and interpretation. And in fact that is what American cultural diplomats did. In the era of the mass circulation of images, they tried to keep track of the response to American photographs and to massage the message as best they could. But they did more than that. They actively engaged in the production and dissemination of photographic images abroad, with a view to putting the best face on an America that was at times, in more ways than one, offensive.

Photography and Cultural Diplomacy

It took the United States a while to find the proper institutional structure for its official cultural diplomacy. A practical middle ground had to be found between conflicting views and demands. Would its purpose be cultural diplomacy in the traditional sense of sponsoring elite cultural events, such as concerts, ballet tours, traveling exhibitions, or the presentation of American life and culture more generally? What would be the proper balance between autonomy of action and its political accountability? If its purpose was information rather than propaganda, what was the line separating the two? How could its recruitment of staff, based on expertise in the cultures and languages of peoples at the receiving end, east and west of the Iron Curtain, be safeguarded from McCarthyite accusations of harboring left-wingers, if not communists, under its wing?

The Smith-Mundt Act of 1948, which formally outlined the government's postwar global information and cultural exchange intentions, as well as President Truman's call for a "Campaign of Truth" to fight the Cold War in 1950, concentrated minds on coordinating the various activities in this area. Several of these went back to World War II days and the Office of War Information (OWI), the Voice of America most prominently among them. The OWI's News and Features Bureau Picture Division after the war had been shifted to the Department of State, where it continued to operate in reduced form. Other programs, such as the Fulbright program for educational exchange, originated in the immediate postwar years. In the face of relentless questioning and intimidation by McCarthy's Permanent Subcommittee on Investigations of the United States Senate, ravaging careers if not lives (one man, Raymond Kaplan, took his own life rather than testify before McCarthy's tribunal), the United States Information Agency (USIA) came into being on August 1, 1953. As one historian of the USIA put it, it took the new agency a year to recover from the pounding delivered during the first three months of 1953.[16]

The agency would not be independent but was organizationally embedded within the State Department. Abroad its representatives, cultural affairs officers, would be stationed within U.S. embassies. Among the means available to USIA for projecting American culture abroad was photography. The International Press Service (IPS) became a core unit in the new agency and would figure prominently in USIA operations through the next four decades. During those years hundreds of thousands of photographs were produced and assembled into photo stories, filmstrips, exhibits, pamphlets, book and magazine reprints, as well as the agency's own monthly magazines, outgrowths of OWI's picture-oriented, *Life* magazine–influenced wartime periodicals. Keying the picture assemblage for the assorted productions was the Photographic Branch (renamed the Visual Materials Branch in the mid-1950s and the Visual Services Branch in the 1970s). The photo files of the branch along with context-providing files, offering raw material for investigating the nature of USIA picture editing and deployment, are now at the National Archives. As stills archivist Nicholas Natanson points out: "Taken as a whole, these USIA series show revealing patterns of thematic inclusion and exclusion. One does not have to be a raging critic of the Cold War establishment to note the constant USIA emphasis, through the decades, on the vitality of the American democratic process, federal government activism, U.S.–Third World educational and cultural exchange, American artistic and technological innovation, cooperation across racial, ethnic, economic, national lines. And one does not have to be a champion of current academic fashion to note the telling USIA silence with regard to the domestic anti-Communist investigations of the 1950s, and the anti-war movement, campus upheavals, the counter-culture, urban riots, the Black Power movement in the 1960s–1970s."[17] Yet blood runs thicker than water. The branch staff reflected continuities with war information agencies in terms of literal holdovers and of representation of women as well as racial and ethnic minorities. They were all hardened professionals who knew a thing or two about the ambiguity and polyvalence of photography in its representation of realities. The possible readings of their photographs were manipulated by the branch through captioning devices and cropping techniques, or, as also happened, photographers were sent on assignments with advance scripting by USIA picture editors. Racial subject matter posed particular challenges for visual shapers and reshapers. In quantitative terms the photographic commitment to black-related subjects was considerable, even before black journalist Carl Rowan's 1964–1965 tenure as USIA director. In qualitative terms picture personnel sought ways to highlight the changing racial environment without at the same time conveying impressions of chaos, rage, or the lingering past. As Natanson reminds us, selectivity was crucial. Among Shelby Smith's photographs of the 1963 March on Washington, there were pictures showing a wide array of signs, crowd angles, and collective body language, enhancing the pictures' openness to different readings. Tellingly, the images receiving the widest circulation focused most closely on the safer themes: interracial unity (for the pamphlet *To Join Hands* and the picture story "Good Will Marks the Washington March") or on individual faces of inspiration (for the picture story "Faces of the March"). For the frequent photo stories touching on the everyday lives of American blacks, advance scripting came into play. As Joseph O'Donnell, former Marine Corps photographer, recalls: "With other kinds of assignments, we usually didn't have written instructions—the propaganda angle was pretty much understood. But with the racial subject, there would be these warnings. For instance, if you came upon blacks and whites working together, you were never supposed to show the white seeming to be above the black, ordering him around; that wouldn't go over well abroad."[18] Staff cameraman Yuki King, on assignment to do a 1967 story on teenage grocery baggers at a Washington, D.C., supermarket, was given the following instruction by *Topic Magazine* picture editor Ellen Kemper: "Safeway tells us that both Negro and white kids work at the . . . store. We'd like to show both in the picture. We also want to suggest that many kids work. So you should shoot down the line of checkout counters, showing a row of kids at work. Please make sure that the youngest and most attractive are in the foreground, and that at least two Negroes appear in the foreground."[19]

In spite of such guidelines and the technical means of controlling the message by tampering with it, in spite also of the fact that the USIA branch photographers were knowing and willing participants in visual manipulations, they were not, as I already suggested, the "willing executioners" of a grand scheme of Cold War propaganda. As creative professionals they had much too keen an eye for the ironic margins where a manifest story produces its own subversive reading. They managed to generate images that, in aesthetic or thematic terms, pushed beyond public relations predictability. Many USIA photographs, regardless of their official auspices and propaganda purpose, contribute to our understanding of events, personalities, trends. In the case of photographer and editor Yoichi Okamoto, to give just one example, the trajectory of his career suggests the potential of the USIA for cultivating creativity. The compositional and thematic experiments, the brooding visions pursued in his late 1940s–early 1950s army and USIA work in Austria (there is a gripping picture of a repatriated prisoner of war walking home with Christmas parcels) pointed forward to his edgy, haunting studies of President Johnson for USIA and later work for the Environmental Protection Agency, when he would take a cold look at "the wanton profusion of free enterprise" and the depressing eyesores it created.[20]

When we also take into account the related photographic operation at the State Department—the "mother agency" from which the USIA emerged at midcentury, and to which it returned at century's end— there was a further respect in which the visual propaganda program contributed more than propaganda. Following the USIA split-off, the State Department developed a parallel central picture file devoted to diplomatic officials and events, ultimately encompassing more than 214,000 images over five decades. Keying the growth of still picture activities within the State Department's Visual Services Division was a former New Deal photographer, James Stephen Wright, who, when he became Photography Branch chief in 1954, found himself in a unique position at the State Department: a black administrator in one of the most racially conservative, convention-bound agencies in the nation's capital. Wright helped to bring in, and promote, black photographers Robert McNeill and Whitney Keith. Between them, these black photographers accounted for over one-third of the more than 110,000 images generated by the State Department from the end of the 1940s to the mid-1970s. As significant as the photographic output was Wright's insistence on breaking with the New Deal and OWI assumption that black photographers were to deal primarily with black subject matter. Wright's approach set an important precedent for other civilian agencies. It set off a sequence of connections that, for instance, made possible the creative work of the current black photographer Gerald Dean, who, while working for the Department of Housing and Urban Development, took an ironic, if not provocative, shot of Vice President George Bush seated, with legs crossed and resting his head on his hand, under a commanding black-and-white portrait of Martin Luther King, Jr.[21]

"The Family of Man" and the Brussels Expo

In his application for a Guggenheim Fellowship, awarded in 1952, black photographer Roy DeCarava wrote: "I want to photograph Harlem through the Negro people . . . at work, at play, in the streets, talking, kidding, laughing. . . . I want to show the strength, the wisdom, the dignity of the Negro people. Not the famous and the well-known, but the unknown and the unnamed, thus revealing the roots from which springs the greatness of all human beings. . . . I want a creative expression, the kind of penetrating insight and understanding of Negroes which I believe only a Negro photographer can interpret."[22] DeCarava's affirmative rhetoric sits astride two discourses that at the time he wrote his application were diverging, two views of authority and authenticity in documentary photography. From one perspective his claims on behalf of the exclusive authority of black photographers in representing black life seem like a throwback to the days when black photographers, working for the Farm Security Administration (FSA) and the OWI in the late 1930s and early 1940s, or later as photojournalists, were, as a matter of course, assigned the documentation and reportage of black life. They seem like a reversal of what Robert McNeill throughout his career, from his early work for the Writers' Project—*The Negro in Virginia*—to his purposely "color-blind" work as chief of the State Department's Photographic Branch, had been striving to achieve, to break out of a professional compartmentalization based on race. Yet there is a different experiential feel to the two positions. DeCarava's claim for the authenticity of photographic representation based on the empathy of shared experience was no longer a matter of filling a niche imposed and defined by others. His was a personal choice, much like McNeill's. Only their choices took each photographer in a different direction. DeCarava in fact very much reflected a more general trend in American photography at the time, away from the genre of social documentation and its implied political agency toward a more inward-looking, subjective, ambivalent, and more purely photographic aesthetics. More than that, he also foreshadowed views much more commonly held in the later age of cultural and identity politics.

DeCarava, as I said, was straddling positions and trends. Insisting that he would picture a reality that "only a Negro photographer can interpret," DeCarava touched at the same time on a universalist theme—"the roots from which springs the greatness of all human beings." This language is reminiscent of Edward Steichen's grand, though concisely worded, vision that inspired what is arguably the most important and influential photographic exhibition ever mounted: the 1955 "Family of Man" show at the Museum of Modern Art in New York. Steichen had sponsored DeCarava's Guggenheim application, and a few years later in his 1955 MOMA show he included several of DeCarava's pictures among the 503 photographs finally selected from a total of over two million. The photographs in the show came from sixty-eight countries; the photographers who took them—273 men and women—were "amateurs and professionals, famed and unknown," as Steichen explained in his introduction to the exhibition catalog.[23] The exhibition, according to Steichen, "was conceived as a mirror of the universal elements and emotions in the everydayness of life—as a mirror of the essential oneness of mankind throughout the world."

It was a grand vision and a grand dream for a man who in a distinguished career as a photographer had witnessed and recorded war in the Pacific theater of operations and who, as director of the Photography Department of the Museum of Modern Art, had exhibited war photographs there in three different shows. His hopes, when taking war photographs and exhibiting them, were typical of Steichen, the humanist and optimist. Showing the face of war to the general public would, he hoped, strengthen their innate pacifism. But as he found out to his chagrin, the confrontation with war photographs left people relatively unaffected. Having seen the show, they forgot about it once they returned to their daily round of life. Hopes like Steichen's are being dashed time and time again, as Susan Sontag has recently reminded us.[24] In a reversal of tack to reach the same goal Steichen adopted a more inspirational approach in organizing his "Family of Man."

Ideas of the oneness of mankind, of mankind forming a single but diverse family, were current at the time. In fact, as a direct precursor and possible inspiration to Steichen, the *Ladies' Home Journal* had run a series of twelve-page spreads in 1948 and 1949 titled "People Are People the World Over," using photographs produced by the independent Magnum picture agency. The series was the idea of Robert Capa, one of Magnum's founding members. Capa had also, in a similar spirit, traveled with John Steinbeck to the Soviet Union in the summer of 1947. Capa spent an entire month in the kolkhoz of Sortschenko, photographing people in their everyday settings, embracing them in his quasi-familial glance. The trip resulted in a book, *A Russian Journal,* with texts by Steinbeck accompanying Capa's photographs.[25] Its dust jacket tells us: "One of the world's best-loved authors, accompanied by one of the world's most famous photographers, meets the Russian people face to face. Refreshingly, informally, and without political bias, he tells how they live and what they think." At a time when Cold War animosities were building up, the book may have seemed strangely out of place, continuing a view of the Russian people as allies in the global struggle against fascism. It is reminiscent more of the images presented by Frank Capra in *The Battle of Russia,* part of his World War II "Why We Fight" series of documentary films, than of postwar attempts at casting the Soviets as the new totalitarian enemy.

More generally, such attempts at presenting the world's population in terms of familial bonds were a projection onto the global scale of a frantic quest in which Americans were collectively engaged during the postwar years. Patterns of exclusion and discrimination had given way to forms of inclusion and acceptance of cultural variety within America, with minorities joining the mainstream of American life on a scale not seen before. Jointly they set out to explore and redefine the bonds that held them all together as a nation, in unity and diversity. The organizing metaphor in much of this public endeavor was the family, itself a stage of unifying bonds and diverging individualities. Photography, particularly in the *Life* magazine photo essay mold, allowed people to include others within a quasi-familial glance, or more precisely to exchange glances with them as so many members of an extended family. The experience most likely goes back to the populist enthusiasm of the 1930s, producing its vast body of photographs under government auspices, most particularly those of the Farm Security Administration (FSA). As one telling title of a 1937 publication of photographs by Margaret Bourke-White put it: *You Have Seen Their Faces.* Making people see has been the driving force behind all documentary photography hoping to create communal bonds and feelings of empathy, to bring society's drift toward the anonymity of what sociologists had begun to call "secondary relations" back to the quality of primary relations. If the latter are characterized by their face-to-face nature, photography was thought to be the ideal tool to reduce the vastness of society to individual faces, expressively telling their individual stories.

The professional canon of photography in the postwar years had begun to move away from this populist impulse, promoting instead the fine-art potential of photography and the individuality of the photographer as artist, but Steichen went against the grain. He couldn't care less; he had seen it all. Having been close to Alfred Stieglitz in the early years of the century, having established a name for himself as a fine-art photographer in the pictorialist mode, he had then ventured into commercial photography and war documentary. On the occasion of his nineti-eth birthday, celebrated with a grand fête at New York's Plaza Hotel, Steichen had this much (or little) to say: "When I first became inter-ested in photography . . . [m]y idea was to have it recognized as one of the fine arts. Today I don't give a hoot in hell about that. The mission of photography is to explain man to man and each man to himself." Given his age, he may be forgiven for not using gender-free language, but his point is clear. There was a feisty humanism in his mature views that guided him when mounting the MoMA "Family of Man" show.

Does the family metaphor, which structured the show, mean that it held politics and ideology at arm's length in the highly charged political climate of the 1950s? Some critics have argued precisely that. Such a view even led Susan Sontag in *On Photography* curtly to dismiss the en-tire venture. Others tend to disagree. In fact we might argue that the idea of the essential oneness of mankind underlying the show's world-view chimed well with a prevailing humanist liberalism, a One World enthusiasm, as it inspired parts of the foreign policy establishment. Nel-son Rockefeller may be the crucial connection here. He combined many roles, ranging from sponsor of the arts to architect of America's cultural diplomacy. He had been central to establishing the USIA; he was also involved in a number of covert, CIA-sponsored cultural projects abroad; and as an art lover he sponsored the foreign exhibitions of America's avant-garde in painting. He had been president of MoMA from 1946 on, and at the time of the opening of Steichen's show was special assis-tant to the president of the United States. In his address at the opening of "The Family of Man" Rockefeller praised Steichen's ability "to com-municate his deep sympathy and love for man, his contagious zest for the flowing stream of life, and his undeviating respect for the inherent dignity of the human spirit." He concluded with a quotation from Pres-ident Eisenhower that called for hope, not fear, in those Cold War years.[26] Rockefeller recognized the potential uses of Steichen's message for foreign policy purposes and was instrumental in getting the USIA to adopt the exhibition and send it abroad, while financially cosponsoring the enterprise.

In hindsight Rockefeller's and Eisenhower's words may strike us as faint praise. Yet at the time, with McCarthyism at its apogee, with nuclear fears, with the anxieties of a society in quest of its own self, Steichen's message of hope and his family focus were timely. He may well have felt above the fray—to quote David Riesman's terms coined at the time to describe America's "lonely crowd," Steichen was not Riesman's other-directed man but, if anything, Riesman's autonomous man. Yet the McCarthyist spirit of persecution and character assassination had touched his intimate circle. His collaborator on the show, as well as brother-in-law, Carl Sandburg, poet and historian, a man of Lincolnian affinities and eloquence, had since the 1930s had his own FBI file. By 1958, three years after "The Family of Man" premiered at MoMA, the FBI upgraded Sandburg's status in their records to "Internal Security-C" (for communist).[27] Sandburg most likely had made Steichen aware of Lincoln's use of the metaphor of the family of man. He wrote the prologue to the show's catalog and was consulted frequently regarding overall themes, assembling captions (along with Dorothy Norman) from world literature to accompany the thematic grouping of photographs, from courtship, marriage, childbirth, child rearing, enjoyment, strife, formal education, work, and old age to death.

Steichen's intended audience may have been the broad American middle class rather than the typically more sophisticated 1950s visitor to a museum's hallowed space, and his chosen view of photography may have been middlebrow, accommodating a lay audience's views of photographs as pictures of the world rather than aesthetic objects in their own right, but his ideas concerning the construction of a text from the various elements were definitely modernist. They may have been inspired by a 1938 display of FSA photographs in New York's Grand Central Terminal. That show made full use of the exhibition space, allowing its audience, mostly commuters, to wander among images printed in various sizes and to pick their own path through the exhibition. But a more important influence was the exhibition theories of the Bauhaus designer Herbert Bayer, who in the late 1930s had brought from Germany to the Museum of Modern Art his techniques exploiting peripheral vision, three-dimensional collage, and engineered perspectives to create an overwhelming effect on the viewer. Steichen had used such ideas in his earlier exhibits. For "The Family of Man" the floor plan was designed by the young architect Paul Rudolph, making for a similarly daring break with the museum tradition of linear displays along museum walls.[28] What Steichen produced was an installation, an artwork in its own right. He turned two-dimensional display into three-dimensional space, suggesting a flow along the images while allowing for multiple vision. If

Steichen's hopes for the universal language and appeal of photographs resembled the appeal of music, the two media were merged in the image of a Peruvian flute player, displayed at several stations in the exhibition, his inviting eyes leading viewers along like a pied piper.

Although the overall narrative strategy was that of a photo album, with people playing, making love, mothering, there were jarring themes of people fighting, making war. There were many disturbing images subtly subverting a message of brotherly love. There was the image of a lynched American black man (not sent on tour abroad, or included in the catalog); there was most importantly the huge, transparent photograph of a nuclear explosion, the only picture in full color, toward the end of the exhibition. This was the single most compelling image addressing the collective fears of the time, shared by Americans and non-Americans alike, giving their poignancy to the extended family bonds that the show evoked. This picture, meant symbolically to overhang the entire display, also was not included in the catalog, nor was it in the show on its Japanese tour. These are only a few indications of why it is unfair to judge the exhibition by its catalog, as so many critics have apparently done. Most importantly, though, the catalog once again reduces to linear display what the show's design so daringly rejected. As Eric Sandeen argues convincingly, if one wishes to do justice to Steichen's ideas, one must mentally reconstruct the show as a three-dimensional installation. Also, one has to see and understand the MoMA show at its particular moment in American history or, for that matter, during the time it traveled under USIA auspices from the mid-1950s to the early 1960s, against the backdrop of America's cultural diplomacy in the Cold War.[29]

Until I returned to the "Family of Man" exhibition's photographs in preparation for this book, I had not seen them for years. My sister has a copy of the catalog from the time the show was on display in Amsterdam's Museum of Modern Art, the Stedelijk Museum. The year was 1956. I was all of sixteen years old. I missed the show but eagerly went over the pictures in the catalog. Returning to them now, I was struck by the fact that I vividly remembered most of them as if I had last seen them a week ago. Whatever Steichen's authorial intent, this must be kept in mind. So many photographs in the show are simply very powerful. If the show taught one thing to its spectators, it was the power of the medium. For many it was their first exposure to it. Ever since, many must have looked more consciously at photographs than before. The exhibition also helped to raise the status of photography, particularly in countries less receptive than the United States to the new medium, with less of a history in creating an infrastructure, through galleries, museums, college curricula, magazines, and journals, for the medium to flourish. In that, unintended, sense, the show offered an education and made for the emancipation of photography as a recognized art form in many countries outside the United States. Much as individual authorship, to the chagrin of many in America's photographic community, may have been submerged in Steichen's assemblage, the photographs individualized themselves and spoke unmistakably with the voice of their makers. At the same time, as an assemblage, it was representative of a great many different styles and genres of photography. There was work by photojournalists (many photographs in the show came from *Life* magazine's photo files and had been published before); other work came from the tradition of the social documentary, in the FSA style or the more radically left-wing Photo League style. There was work by up-and-coming young photographers, such as Roy DeCarava, Robert Frank, Diane Arbus, or Gary Winogrand, who were soon to leave Steichen's warm familial embrace and move in different directions. There were many non-American photographers, some famous, some unknown. The show was a veritable panopticon, not only of the family of man, but of the ways that photography has to include them in a familial gaze. Steichen's approach was modular and may be seen as illustrative of a typically American way with culture.[30] He took photographs from many sources, by many authors, and recombined and recontextualized them to make them serve his message. Yet, as I cannot emphasize enough, there was a multivocality, if not a multifocality, in the assembled body of pictures that may well have affected the way spectators read the exhibition. It is impossible to reconstruct what the millions of spectators worldwide, in their many cultural settings, with their many individual concerns and perspectives, took home with them, what exactly the joys of their cultural consumption had been.

Yet, in America and abroad, there were many critical minds interposing themselves between the show and its individual spectators. Art critics, like culture critics more generally, see their role as speaking authoritatively on behalf of the public or to educate and guide its perceptions and interpretations. In the United States, as Vicky Goldberg and Robert Silberman summarize, Steichen's efforts were criticized from two directions.[31] One had to do with the disregard for the artistic autonomy of the individual artists involved in the show. Ansel Adams, although included in the show with a few large prints of Western landscapes, complained that Steichen had not supported the fine print aesthetic. The photographers represented had not been allowed to make their own prints but had simply been asked to provide negatives. The other major criticism of the exhibition was that photographs were being used to illustrate an ideological vision and message typical of postwar liberalism. I have addressed some of this criticism above. But even in more sympathetic reviews of the show that appear in recent writings on photography we find echoes of the earlier critique, though cast in more contemporary critical language.

Marianne Hirsch, for one, takes a fresh look at "The Family of Man" and places the show in the context of her explorations of family photographs. She recognizes many features of the genre in the exhibition, such as the familial gaze, the specularity in the exchange of glances, with people being looked at looking back, engaging the viewer in conversation. Others, for instance Alan Sekula, have seen this as a ploy "for the collapse of the political into the familial,"[32] and they have sided with those critics, such as Susan Sontag and Roland Barthes, who see the show as a sentimental conjuring trick, naturalizing the representation of mankind in disregard of historical context and politics. Hirsch sees things differently. Quasi-familial as the gaze of the exhibition may seem to be, there is a fundamental imbalance in the direction of the gaze. Hirsch recognizes an underlying imperialism in the exhibition; what it presents is an established European and American way of looking at the world and ordering it in an overall picture. People from the third world are present in the show, but never through self-representation. They are the objects of a Western gaze. Thus, Hirsch reintroduces politics in her reflections. She wonders what the show would have looked like if third-world people had trained their lenses, had they had any, on themselves and on the West. It would have restored a balance in the exchange of glances through the empowerment of the camera lens. Now, as she puts it, "the space of identification [offered by Steichen's show] is the space enjoyed by the Western European and European-American bourgeois nuclear family,"[33] a space that others could only vicariously share by look-ing in from outside. Precisely such a sense of outsidership, of having been turned into spectacle for Western eyes to behold, may have been behind the protest of an African student in Moscow. He tore up several pictures when the show was on display there, claiming it represented the third world as poor and primitive compared with the West. Yet others, in Moscow and elsewhere, saw it in a different light. Hirsch's reading seems unduly reductive of the options for identification that the exhibi-tion provided. In a telling digression she acknowledges as much, when she ponders how she would have viewed the show if it had come to Ru-mania, where she grew up. "Had my family and I seen the exhibit, how-ever, we would certainly have identified with its message of 'universal brotherhood.'" Her parents' Austrian-Jewish upbringing on Heinrich Heine and Stefan Zweig, their recent history of persecution, and their minority status as German-speaking Jews in Rumania would have made them "ideal visitors to the 'Family of Man.'" "Even the contradictions in our mentality would have been reflected in the images: the belief in human equality, on the one hand, and, on the other, our own sense of cultural superiority as 'Western Europeans' displaced in the Balkans . . . as well as our fragile bourgeois comfort, all correspond to the mentality of Steichen's 'human family.' The space of identification is the space en-joyed by the Western European and European-American bourgeois nu-clear family, a space to which we were close enough that, by the logic of the family romance, we could imagine, desire ourselves into it. In the aftermath of the Nazi deportations, the image of a close-knit nuclear family would itself have inspired us as . . . a sanctuary to be cherished and protected. An ideal made up of humanity, familiality, and universal communication would surely have found resonance."[34] In this exercise in the joys of vicarious identification with the show's message, of people looking in from outside, Hirsch suggests at least one of the many ways in which people the world over might have enjoyed the show, in private control of their individual reading.

The ultimate empowerment, as I argued before, is in the eye of the beholder, in the choices he or she makes identifying with all these open faces from all over the world looking us in the eye. The enjoyment of the millions of spectators is, in the final analysis, the black box containing all the mysteries of appropriation, private perception, and identification. No critic, interposing him- or herself in the field of vision, has the authority to speak on behalf of the audience without asking them. That, as I see it, is what the critical empowerment of the spectator is all about.

As for the interaction between spectators and the many faces represented in the show's photographs, "The Family of Man" has spawned its own progeny. There is a rich album of photographs showing spectators immersing themselves in the photographs in an exchange of glances, establishing, as it were, eye contact with fellow members of the Family of Man. Many of these photographs were taken at the behest of the USIA as the show was touring the world, as proof and testimony of its public appeal and appreciation. Edward Steichen himself contributed to this collection with photographs he took when the exhibition was on show in Moscow.[35] Such documents give a visual hint at least of the ways in which individual spectators communed with individual photographs. What helped foreign audiences empathize was the fact that photographs from sixty-eight different countries were on display. Thus, in one telling case, we can see Queen Juliana of the Netherlands, easily the most motherly of monarchs, viewing Dutch photographer Emmy Andriesse's picture of an elderly rural couple, fellow Dutch people, illustrating Ovid's dictum, "We two are a multitude."[36]

Much of the criticism that we touched on so far was in response to the original MoMA exhibition or the accompanying catalog. There is little reference to the Cold War context other than its inclusion of the threat of nuclear annihilation. The threat was generalized, though, not explicitly connected to the agency of parties confronting each other in the Cold War. If agency was suggested, it was of a countervailing kind. One of the final images in the exhibit shows the United Nations General Assembly as the site for "heads of families" to sort out their differences peacefully. To the extent that the show's implied political frame of mind was criticized, as in Hirsch's critique of the imperial gaze that structured the representation of humanity, we recognize much older lines of a critique of ideology. Revisiting earlier mass cultural events such as the Chicago 1893 World's Fair or Buffalo Bill's Wild West show, historians have consistently pointed out the implied strategies of self-presentation of Western civilization, European and American, as the pinnacle of progress and development, with the rest of the world seen as mired in earlier, more primitive stages in the onward march of civilization.[37]

Clearly, from the moment that the USIA took the show under its wing and sent it traveling, its use as Cold War propaganda affected the framework of perception. Not surprisingly, some reviews of the show at its various stops in European cities addressed the propaganda issue more explicitly than had earlier American comments. Yet in general the show was a great public success. Its stature was enhanced by the fact that in many places museums hosted the show. Press comments on the whole reflected the public response. As noted above, the positive reception of the exhibition may in part be due to the fact that many European countries were represented in the images, often by photographers from those countries. This helped people meaningfully to connect to the larger message of the show from their own national perspectives and affiliations. Yet, to the extent that press reviewers were aware of the USIA auspices, some set out to explore the Americanness of a message that aimed at being universal. Allergic as many Europeans, particularly those of a left-wing bent, had been to what they perceived as American attempts to set the terms of the confrontation with the Soviet Union, they chose to draw on older repertoires of cultural anti-Americanism. Thus, they recognized in Steichen's message a sentimentalism and a naive optimism to be dismissed as typically American, far removed from an allegedly greater European sophistication and tragic sense of the human condition. Many had been the voices in Europe, from Spengler to Sartre, claiming that American culture missed the European sense of the tragic. To people such as these the message remained essentially alien, that is, American. Hardly ever was the critique of the show's underlying ideology more original than this. Nor did it truly speak on behalf of a mass audience's enthusiastic response.

As the many reports from USIA posts to Washington amply illustrate, "The Family of Man" was a smashing success wherever it went.[38] Although the USIA auspices were always openly acknowledged, what may have furthered its reception was the collaboration with local sponsors, such as leading art museums. Thus, in the Netherlands, the Amsterdam Stedelijk Museum, a pioneering modern art institution, hosted the show. In addition a leading Amsterdam newspaper, *Het Parool*, sponsored and advertised the show. Founded during World War II as an underground resistance paper, it had become a leading voice in the early Cold War years of militant social democratic anticommunism. It was precisely the sort of European intellectual voice that America's cultural diplomacy, openly or under CIA cover, coveted.[39]

There is one further way in which USIA auspices may have affected the reading of Steichen's exhibition. The USIA role was not that of a mere travel agent for the show. Although the agency never tampered with Steichen's overall message, it did on occasion change the context in which the show was put on display, most clearly perhaps in Moscow. There, two strategies of American self-representation in cultural diplomacy came together: that of the international trade fair, showing the plethora of consumer goods that had come to direct Americans' collective pursuit of happiness; and that of the liberal, One World view presented by "The Family of Man." The famous kitchen debate between Khrushchev and Nixon may have recontextualized the stakes of the Cold War rivalry, turning it into a race between the superpowers for greatest consumer satisfaction. It also affected the reading of "The Family of Man," showing humanity on its way to the joys of the consumers' republic, as seen through American eyes.

Remarkably, with the Cold War behind us, the diverse history of readings of Steichen's "Family of Man" continues. The show has found its final, and permanent, home in Steichen's country of origin, Luxembourg. It is on permanent display in the castle of Clervaux, in a reconstruction of the form in which it toured so many countries for so long. Rather than as a mere relic, or a posthumous tribute to Steichen as its *auctor intellectualis,* eliciting nostalgia for its remembered meanings, it goes on to stimulate new readings. A notable recent collection of essays revisits the show in an acknowledgment of its continuing power to speak to current concerns and anxieties. In one essay Viktoria Schmidt-Linsenhoff engages the exhibit in terms not of its Cold War relevance but of what it has to say about the European trauma of the Holocaust, or the Shoa as she prefers to call it. When she reencountered the exhibit at Clervaux, one picture with which she was very familiar because of her earlier work on photography by the Nazi henchmen "took her breath away." The photograph, from the Stroop report on the destruction of the Warsaw ghetto, was presented in such a way as to conceal and at the same time highlight the absence of the Shoa as the invisible center of the exhibition. It led her to a reinterpretation of "The Family of Man" as a symptom of the legacy of the Shoa in conjunction with the trauma theories in the arts and humanities that have increasingly come under discussion since the mid-1990s. Given the mass exposure to pictures of Nazi terror following the liberation of concentration camps in the final days of World War II, the relative silence of Steichen's exhibit regarding the Nazi infamy appeared as only one case of the more general repression of a collective mass memory of this ultimate horror. Following the early flood of photographs and books documenting the Nazi horrors, a silence set in enveloping both the survivors and the body of former fellow citizens to which they had returned. There was a shared sense of picking up the thread of life that had been ruptured by the war, of resuming life as if nothing had intervened to break it. But the repression of trauma comes at a terrible price. From the late 1960s onward there was a return of the repressed with a vengeance. Many succumbed to what came to be known as the concentration camp syndrome. Some managed creatively to translate the return of traumatic memories into writing, as in the case of Dutch author Gerhard Durlacher. Following an attempt to return to normal civilian bourgeois life in the Netherlands as a survivor of Nazi concentration camps, only psychiatric treatment helped him to veer back to life from a deep depression and to harness the flood of returned memories in magisterial writing. He, like many others such as French filmmaker Claude Lanzman, brought back to public awareness what the larger public in Europe and America had known all along but had chosen to forget.

Edward Steichen mounted his "Family of Man" exhibit at the high point of this collective endeavor in forgetfulness. In his case authorial intent rather than amnesia or the willful repression of traumatic images guided him in the final selection of photographs. In the two years of preparation for the exhibit he must have gone over many of the concentration camp pictures that had circulated widely a mere eight years before. The photographs of Buchenwald, Dachau, and Bergen-Belsen by Margaret Bourke-White, Lee Miller, and George Roger were in the archives from which the majority of the material in the exhibition was taken. Yet, rather than include any of Lee Miller's photographs of heaps of corpses in Dachau, he selected Miller's moving image of a child and a cat as part of the closing section of the exhibition on children. Only one panel, in the section captioned "Man's inhumanity to Man," may have served to trigger the visual archive of the unconscious in the minds of the show's visitors. Two photographs in that section show men, women, and children being led at gunpoint out of the burning Warsaw ghetto before being herded by the Germans to their deaths in the Treblinka extermination camp. A third photograph at the top of the panel was taken in Israel in 1951. It shows a black-haired woman in dark clothing, her emaciated arm raised aloft in a monumental gesture, the fingers eloquently splayed, in a spiritual cry of outrage. The composition gives the impression that this woman is not only bewailing the suffering in the Warsaw ghetto but is triumphing over it. Centrally placed on the panel is a text quoted from George Sand: "Humanity is outraged in me and with me. We must not dissimulate nor try to forget this indignation which is one of the most passionate forms of love." Text and photographs together indicate that the image of the woman is an allegory of the state of Israel, a state whose origins lay in the suffering of innocent victims and which was retrospectively invested with the spirit and dignity of the founding sacrificial victims. Thus recontextualizing the images, Steichen imbues them with new meaning, connecting past trauma with future hopes. In this suturing approach, stitching past and future together, Steichen may at points seem to deny the intervening horror, when, for instance, he shows two pictures by Roman Vishniac and Margaret Bourke-White of Jewish schools in Poland and Czechoslovakia from the 1930s. Steichen's narrative ploy here is rather the soothing creation of a cyclical time of salvation, a circle whose closure consists precisely in salvaging visual traces of a past that otherwise has been violently annihilated.

Thus "The Family of Man" deals with the Shoa only through subtle recontextualization, never confronting the viewer directly with Nazi atrocity photographs. Yet, as Viktoria Schmidt-Linsenhoff argues, there are ways in which we can see Steichen's entire project as addressing issues of racism and genocide. If the exhibition can be considered the qualitative pinnacle of a stylistic genre known as human interest photography, Steichen at the same time deconstructed the genre. As a genre, it had discovered the particular and the nonrepresentative, the anecdotal. Steichen, though, chose to bend it toward his neohumanist purposes. He rhythmically punctuated the sequences of images of everyday life with archaic natural images of biblical force, obliterating the sensitivity to the "human interest" in the photographs. Thus, as Schmidt-Linsenhoff puts it: "This systematic inversion from the particular to the universal, from profane to sacred, from visual serendipity to divine plan for creation, clearly points to the horror unleashed by the 'senseless destruction of life for its own sake,' a horror which the exhibition addresses without showing the 'horrific images.'"[40] Steichen's entire vision can then be understood as one frantic attempt to send out a message of "Never Again."

The Brussels Expo of 1958

Whatever its context, "The Family of Man," in terms of its soft-sell use of cultural diplomacy, proved a huge success. Not always, though, did the power of photographs as human documents guarantee the success of their use for cultural diplomacy. There is one case of a dismal failure that should be mentioned here. Ironically, the attempt this time was more daring than the relatively safe approach of the "Family of Man" exhibition. The occasion was the 1958 Brussels World's Fair. Shortly before, photographs had dominated front pages of newspapers all over Europe, showing the ugly face of white racism in the American South. Little Rock had put itself on the map, deeply affecting the reading of American race relations in the eyes of many Europeans. Iconic photographs of dignified black students, surrounded by hissing white faces, were reminiscent of late medieval depictions of the defamation of Christ. Clearly, America's projection of its self-image for the millions of visitors to the World's Fair could not simply ignore this. It was decided that, in an annex to America's stunning pavilion, photo collages would be mounted to address a number of current issues that were of concern to Americans and their government. The general caption would read: "Unfinished Work." If America in its main pavilion could rightfully pride itself on its many achievements, the side show's organizers chose to acknowledge that not everything was perfect but that Americans were working on it.

As more than one author tells the story,[41] a group around Walt Whitman Rostow at MIT was put in charge of this project. He was then working on his "noncommunist manifesto," *Stages of Economic Growth,* and was apparently willing to apply his developmental views of human societies to the United States as well, practicing what he preached. The show opened in Brussels and was well received. Concerted efforts by southern politicians, however, managed to kill the project. The show was closed and reopened after a few weeks with a new item of unfinished business, a public health exhibit organized by the Department of Health, Education, and Welfare. It did not go unnoticed in the European press. The ignominious retreat was duly covered. As an effort in cultural diplomacy, which had favored openness over stealth, it was a disaster.

SIX ◎ AN EYE FOREIGN EYE

Un-American Photography and the Cold War

IS THERE SUCH A THING as un-American photography? The answer depends on whom you ask. But certainly at the height of the McCarthyite anticommunist crusade there were many who developed a keen eye for un-American qualities where no one had seen these before. In the arts, writers, painters, photographers, and filmmakers now found themselves under scrutiny for potentially un-American messages carried by their work. As just one example, Robert Capa, U.S. citizen since 1946, saw his passport canceled in 1948. His work, never before seen as overly or overtly political, was now deemed un-American. He had photographed the Spanish Civil War from the Republican side, the side that many international left-wingers sympathized with or had actively supported. Even his patently unpolitical view of simple Russian farmers, published in book form as *A Russian Journal,* as well as in a special edition of *Ladies' Home Journal*—as all-American a magazine as they come— now was seen as proof of Capa's left-wing sympathies. He was made to pay for them, like so many others whose cosmopolitanism and internationalism made them suspect in the eyes of those who defined America in more parochial terms. This chapter will explore the highly charged political atmosphere of 1950s America and the way this affected the reading of photography.

Recent scholarship has brought greater nuance and subtlety to our understanding of Edward Steichen's "Family of Man" exhibition. Among recent studies, Lili Bezner's *Photography and Politics in America: From the New Deal into the Cold War* is arguably the most convincing in its reconstruction of the show as an ideological balancing act, which she accomplishes through a superb close reading of the show's individual photographs.[1] She concludes that "[u]pon deeper reflection subversive cracks in the supposedly ideal surface of the 'Family of Man' appear. In a few instances, both visually and philosophically, Steichen took risks with the show. He succeeded in bridging diverse ideological branches in an exhibition that enjoyed endorsement by socialist as well as conservative journals."[2]

Despite the tremendous tensions between the United States and the Soviet Union, not one of the thirteen Soviet images is situated within any "negative" section of the show. Rather, they integrate Soviet otherness into the intended oneness of Steichen's vision. As Bezner makes clear, ambivalent but critical photographs are embedded within a preponderance of palatable, favorable, and positive images, revealing a subtextual effort to counter and sometimes contradict the conservative myths and stereotypes of the time. The show is not completely, in every moment, optimistic about humanity. Some themes and images in "The Family of Man" conflict with reigning stereotypes of the 1950s American Dream. Photographs include scenes of the dead, the unempowered, racial discrimination, and gender conflicts, among other potent issues. Instances of Steichen's questioning the mainstream values held dear by so many Americans are more numerous than viewers today may perceive.

The narrative of the exhibition, and by extension of the show's catalog, does not simply reflect the Cold War status quo. As Bezner reminds us: "The images at times explode against one another in a seesaw of liberal versus conservative values."[3] But she points out, following a survey of later critical comments, that photographs with political content have been repeatedly dismissed and effectively silenced by the critical, intellectual community of later decades. Given the suppression, even destruction, of documentary photographers such as Ben Shahn, whose overtly political art and activism landed him in a House Un-American Activities (HUAC) court, or Sid Grossman, who was under FBI surveillance, Steichen's effort at communicating traditional social documentary ideals, as nuanced as they were in "The Family of Man," might be seen as a survival tactic within the repressive sociopolitical context of the 1950s. His inclusion of the work of several of these "suspect," left-wing photographers was an act of solidarity as well as an affirmation of his faith in the documentary power of photography. One example is the haunting image of a black mother in Florida, a 1950 photograph by Consuelo Kanaga. She had internalized documentary ideals during a career going back to her 1930s work for the *Daily Worker* and the *New Masses,* as well as for the WPA. Her hopeful, activist sense of photography's social mission speaks clearly from her image of the Florida mother. Thin and exhausted, impoverished but alive, the mother shelters her small charges. It was an image that suited Steichen's vision of the world's extended, persevering family. Yet it may not have been the image that Americans preferred to see held up as a mirror of their vaunted way of life.

Consuelo Kanaga's work was included in the 1948 show "This Is the Photo League," the last public display of a genre of left-wing social documentary as produced by the Photo League. As early as 1947 the Photo League was blacklisted as a communist front. Many members, most of them New Yorkers, most of them poor, second-generation Jews, had started work in the much more supportive political climate of the 1930s. The Depression more generally may be seen as the high water mark for photography in the social documentary mode. Under government auspices, such as those of the Farm Security Administration and several other government agencies, a generation of photographers had come into its own that took its inspiration more from the work of Lewis Hine than from the self-styled father of American fine-art photography, Alfred Stieglitz. To the extent that a canon of American photography had been forming, it was one mostly inspired by Stieglitz, whose authority had dictated inclusion and exclusion. Hine had been out, until his adoption in the 1930s by the younger generation, including both Rooseveltians and left-wingers.

To the left of the government-sponsored documentary work, the Photo League, from the mid-1930s on, had organized more radically left-wing photographers, affiliating with communism or socialism rather than Rooseveltian New Deal ideas. For many radical organizations of the time, the year 1935 proved schismatic. Stalin's terror, unleashed in Moscow against those he saw as rivals in his relentless march to sole and exclusive control of the Communist Party in the Soviet Union, led many on the Left, in Europe and the United States, to break away from Moscow-oriented cultural organizations. Thus, the Photo League emerged from a three-way split of the New York Film and Photo League. The latter had been founded in 1930, but its origins lay in the earlier Workers' Camera Club, which had been active for some years. As the name suggests, it was an organization inspired and supported by Communist organizations. Workers' International Relief, the American chapter of the *Internationale Arbeiterhilfe,* and part of the Communist International (Komintern), sponsored the merger of the Workers' Camera Club with a similar organization, the Labor Defender Photo Group, into the New York Film and Photo League (FPL). The object of the FPL was to make films and photographs to support workers against their bosses, to assert the rights of working people and fight for a better life for them. These movements drew their inspiration from the German worker-photographer movement organized by Will Münzenberg, at the time a central organizer in the Komintern network.[4] They aimed to awaken the working class and train workers in the use of film and photography for the production of politically committed pictures. The FPL also aimed at projecting a positive picture of Soviet achievements in the areas of film and photo production and found inspiration for its work there.

If this brief sketch suggests two different strands—one connecting a group of 1930s photographers back to a self-conscious American photographic discourse with native roots, the other international, taking its artistic and ideological cues from non-American sources—the impression is wrong, as one strand may remind us: Paul Strand. Making worker-oriented, class-consciousness-raising films in the 1930s, reminiscent of what other documentary filmmakers, such as Joris Ivens, did in Europe, Strand had started his career as a photographer whose early work had deeply impressed Stieglitz. In a style of straight photography, avoiding pictorialist manipulations of the image, it showed an artistic sensitivity and drive that Stieglitz could acknowledge as akin to his own. In the 1920s Strand had shot a film of New York, a fascinating document that aimed at catching the mysteries of the bustle, the rhythms, and the energies of a great metropolis. Yet by the 1930s his focus and perspective had changed. In 1935, when the Film and Photo League split apart, Paul Strand formed a production company, Frontier Films. The still photographers, who largely took the side of Frontier Films, formed a new organization, the Photo League. Frontier Films, throughout its existence, was closely allied with the Photo League. Paul Strand, the president of Frontier Films, was also a member of the advisory board of the Photo League and played an important role in its activities until he left for France in 1949, like so many other creative artists seeking refuge abroad from an America caught up in anticommunist persecution.[5]

But there were more than personal connections that straddled the two movements. There were ideological and aesthetic connections as well. Walter Rosenblum, president of the Photo League at the time of its blacklisting in 1947, wrote a piece in the June 1948 issue of the League's journal, *Photo Notes,* in which he said that the League felt a close association with the FSA project. He went on to describe a League-sponsored FSA show and mentioned a lecture Roy Stryker (director of the Historical Section, Division of Information, of the FSA) had given at the League. Stryker, Rosenblum recalled, had based the FSA "on what Lewis Hine had done earlier." This sense of lineage, from Hine to the FSA to the League, had kept social documentary ideals alive. Yet as Anne Tucker has pointed out, at the same time that the League's membership expanded, taking in photographers and critics as diverse as Ansel Adams, Barbara Morgan, Beaumont and Nancy Newhall, W. Eugene Smith, Edward Weston, or FSA photographers such as Jack Delano and John Vachon, there was a gradual shift away from a social to a more personal vision in the Photo League's aesthetic philosophy.[6] An adamant core of members, though, still emphasized the social utility of documentary images. As for the increase in membership and the aesthetic shift, it is possible to see both in connection with the repressive political climate and the blacklisting of the League in December of 1947.

For a long time the work of the Photo League, produced mostly but not solely in New York City, has been overshadowed by the huge documentary production of photographs under government auspices in the 1930s and during World War II. Not until recently have efforts been made to revisit and reassess the Photo League's body of work. In Chicago the Stephen Daiter Gallery organized a show and produced a catalog, *This Was the Photo League.*[7] The Jewish Museum in New York organized an exhibition, "New York: Capital of Photography," where the work of the Photo League was amply represented, and put into context by Max Kozloff in a long essay he contributed to the exhibition's catalog.[8] Finally, Lili Bezner in her recent study tells the story of the Photo League's postwar demise.

One factor in its demise, and in the decline of socially and politically committed documentary photography after the war more generally, had to do with autonomous changes in artists' views of their work and mission. Art was increasingly produced in a highly self-conscious awareness of the act of artistic creation. The world to be expressed in art, whether in music, literature, painting, or photography, was increasingly an inner world. There was a general drift away from the demotic, and vernacular, styles adopted by many artists during the 1930s. In hindsight, the Depression decade looks like an interlude; its democratic enthusiasms as shared by America's artists set it apart from the 1920s as much as from the post–World War II years. Both those eras were characterized more by an avant-garde, modernist, and elitist sense of artistic mission. In other words, in the late 1940s the social realism of documentary photography was beginning to go out of fashion. As I pointed out before, Steichen's exhibition may have been the last salute to the hopes invested in the power of documentary photography.

Yet another, equally important factor was, not the changing artistic climate, but of course the changing political climate. Artists at the time, in whatever creative direction they were moving, were up against tremendous odds. If the successive Roosevelt administrations had pioneered a role as sponsors of artistic production, albeit in the service of the New Deal project, now, after the war, the community of creative artists and arts organizers was faced with an accelerating criticism of art in Cold War America. Philistines now set the agenda, and they ranged from President Truman to members of Congress. Apart from the paranoid extremism of McCarthy and his cronies, mainstream philistinism was given voice by members of Congress such as Republican representative George A. Dondero (Michigan). In his attacks on "communistic" American art, he thundered that it did not "glorify our beautiful country, our cheerful and smiling people, and our material progress." Dondero continued, in this 1949 speech: "Art which does not glorify our beautiful country in plain, simple terms that everyone can understand breeds dissatisfaction. It is therefore opposed to our government, and those who create and promote it are our enemies."[9]

As Lili Bezner has it: "Artists couldn't win. Modern Art was denounced and social realists like Shahn were distrusted. Even though social documentary was realistic, as Dondero preferred, it certainly did not 'glorify' the lives of 'smiling' Americans."[10] Yet "modern art," particularly Abstract Expressionism, may have been able more easily to find powerful sponsors and supporters outside politics than were the social realists of the Photo League. Supported by Rockefeller, the Museum of Modern Art, and the cover provided by the CIA, Abstract Expressionist art was being used to promote Cold War ideals of democratic individuality, placing American modernists in foreign shows. This raises an interesting question. Was the relatively safe haven provided by the private museum world and the covert international network of the CIA a factor in its own right luring American artists away from politically charged documentary styles? If this may have constituted a pull factor, there was also the push factor of the relentless hounding of left-leaning artists. Bezner addresses these questions but cannot truly resolve them. She mentions examples of some leading Photo League members, such as Sid Grossman or Aaron Siskind, who moved toward more abstract, nondocumentary styles of photography. Whether they were driven in those directions by the political climate or autonomously chose to move along with the artistic trends of the time, neither she nor others will probably ever be able to sort out. But the time at which these style changes occurred may at least suggest a tentative answer. When Siskind moved toward modernism and abstraction, he did so relatively early, in an artistic journey that had begun in the late 1930s. In the early postwar years, his associations with Abstract Expressionist painters in New York and Black Mountain College reinforced these experiments. At the same time they estranged him from Photo League colleagues who decried his work as "too arty" and a rejection of the workers' cause. This caused Siskind to leave the League for good.[11] Political pressures were not quite as strong then as they were in Grosman's case. Sid Grosman's aesthetic shifted only during his self-chosen refuge in New England in the 1950s, after he had been publicly named a Communist.

The December 1947 blacklisting of the Photo League by Attorney General Tom Clark led many in the photographic community to express support and outrage. The special January 1948 issue of *Photo Notes* included statements from Rosenblum, a copy of a speech given by an outraged Paul Strand, encouraging letters and telegrams from Dorothea Lange,

Ben Shahn, Jack Levine, Philip Evergood, Edward Weston, and Ansel Adams, and a piece by Rosenblum asking himself and his readers: "Where Do We Go from Here?" The League was not a political organization at all, according to Rosenblum; it was a photographic organization, and the best revenge was to turn it into "a real center of American photography." Barbara Morgan suggested assembling an exhibition of League work in which "the type of photography being attacked—documentary photography" could be presented to a large audience so that the public could "see it and understand its important function in ameliorating evils." With Beaumont Newhall as chairman of the project, this idea would culminate in the 1948 show titled "This Is the Photo League."

Although the Newhalls—Beaumont and his wife, Nancy—were champions of many photographers and styles of photography during their careers, their contributions to *Photo Notes* make it clear that both, but Nancy in particular, still believed in a documentary photography in the classic FSA tradition. The Photo League, as Nancy Newhall wrote again and again, fulfilled this role in its education of photographers. Beaumont Newhall had joined the League, with his wife, in 1947, a good man to have on board for a beleaguered organization. He had enjoyed longer stretches of employment at mainstream institutions, such as the Museum of Modern Art (as librarian, 1935–42, and as curator of photography, 1940–45) and, later, the George Eastman House. Yet in his own historical survey of photography, *The History of Photography* (originally written in 1937, last revised in 1982), Beaumont Newhall consistently ignored the Photo League and its impact on midcentury American photography. The very politics that he and, more particularly, his wife had at some point endorsed, they may have rather washed their hands of in later years. They would not have been the only ones. Membership in the Photo League would become a blemish on one's record as the anticommunist furor in the United States mounted. The Newhalls left the League after a few years. They were not alone. Red-baiting caused many others to run for cover. The Photo League struggled on for a few more years but finally disbanded in 1951. As its final statement put it: "The Photo League is but one of the casualties [of the Cold War], but the fight . . . is far from over." As it turned out, the fight was over. Modernism was on the rise; documentary work continued its gradual decline. The documentary gaze had come to be suspected of being un-American. Its repression was relentless: an eye foreign eye.

Robert Frank's The Americans

Edward Steichen's influential position at the Museum of Modern Art and the catholicity of his taste in photography made him a mentor of young talent irrespective of style or genre. Yet it was probably coincidence rather than intent on Steichen's part that brought two young photographers together in his "Family of Man" show. One was a Swiss immigrant to the United States and already fairly well known, Robert Frank; the other a young Dutch photographer working in Paris and as yet unknown, Ed van der Elsken. Frank, who helped Steichen get in touch with European photographers in preparation for the exhibition, may have known Van der Elsken and introduced him to Steichen. It is the coincidence of their joint appearance in Steichen's international assemblage, more than anything else, though, that leads me to ponder some transatlantic parallels. Both Frank and Van der Elsken moved in the heady atmosphere of two rival bohemian niches: Saint Germain des Prés in Paris and the East Village in New York. Both provided havens for a lifestyle at odds with the stifling conformity of a culture of consumption that had transformed postwar America and, in its American guise, had incited eager emulation in Europe. Of the two places, Paris was probably still the most international, serving as a crossroads for a European avant-garde and its American counterparts. Beat poets and writers spent time in Paris. So did the pioneers of a revolution in jazz music and other avant-garde American talent. Artistic experiment blended with ideas of existentialism to produce a self-image of the artist as a lone pioneer, exploring the depths of his subjectivity to express both individuality and larger truths about human existence. This Parisian Bohemia had cut itself loose from the tired and overwrought political oppositions of the day, as these had hardened around the Cold War division of the world. But, in both its New York and Paris versions, it was a world of despair and angst rather than of joy, although alcohol might briefly alleviate the gloom. In Paris, in a style of grainy, black-and-white photography that broke with the conventional aesthetics of fine-art photography, Van der Elsken feverishly documented life in Saint Germain. He published a selection of his work in the late 1950s in the Netherlands, which caused quite a splash and has become a classic in the history of European photography. Fully immersed as he had been in the lifestyle of the Paris bohemians, with all its grandeur, miseries, and sleaze, his book was a highly private document in addition to being a *document humain*, capturing artistic ferment in Europe at the height of the Cold War. Frank was never as totally immersed in the New York bohemia, yet he began to share its outlook on life and the role of the artist as the fifties progressed. He felt an affinity with the modernism of Abstract Expressionist painters and with existentialist writing (which he knew well). Yet at the same time he had always easily straddled the line separating mainstream photography from its avant-garde version. He had worked as a commercial fashion photographer and had seen his earlier work of a more conventional nature exhibited on various occasions in the New York Museum of Modern Art, selected by his mentor, Edward Steichen. He had collaborated with the old master preparing the "Family of Man" exhibition, although he later spoke disparagingly of it.

Yet what truly established his reputation as the leading new man in American photography, changing its course forever and establishing his myth as the quintessential lone genius, was a project funded by the Guggenheim Foundation (and, again, supported by Steichen among other grandees of American photography such as Walker Evans). The grant for one year, renewed once, allowed him to travel through the United States in much the same way that the FSA photographers before him had done, visualizing Americans of every walk of life, race, and gender, urban and rural, for their fellow Americans. Yet there were important differences in what Frank set out to do. If the FSA project, under Rooseveltian inspiration and the stern guidance of its chief, Roy Stryker, had been Whitmanesque in its intent to restore a communal vision of the American nation (not unlike Steichen's ambition for "The Family of Man"), Frank's view was highly individual, if not idiosyncratic. His gesture was not one of embrace but of cool and distanced, yes, ironic observation. There was less patent empathy in his pictures, more of the sardonic criticism of an outsider looking in through the prism of preconceived ideas. Given his bourgeois, Swiss background, some of these ideas may have gone back to older European repertoires of a cultural critique of America, of its crass materialism, of its idolatry of cars and other consumption items, or of commercialized ideas of female beauty. His ironic parodies of mass culture and expectations positioned Frank clearly as the avant-garde voyeur looking with (European?) disdain at popular culture tastes. In fact, his language in the Guggenheim application had already suggested this. The project would be only "partly documentary in nature: one of its aims is more artistic than the word documentary implies." He stressed that such images would record the observations of "one naturalized American" of a "civilization born here and spreading elsewhere."[12] This was the type of concern that had caused so many Europeans for well over two centuries to observe American civilization at its source and to report back to their various home audiences.

Yet at the same time many of his photographs of race relations in the American South tied in with earlier photographic views produced by Americans. It did not take a European eye to see injustice. Yet Frank's strategy in showing such injustice was more detached and distanced than earlier work in the great American tradition of social documentary photography. His pictures are chilling rather than heartwarming; they use alienation in almost a Brechtian way as a communicative strategy, leading the viewer to observe and reflect rather than empathize. He may have been an "original," yet there is a lineage connecting Frank to the American documentary tradition. He was aware of it and admired much of it, particularly Evans's work. Frank may have sustained documentary ideals while subverting, extending, or enriching them within a new historical context.

By the time he set out on his journey, in 1955, his ideas on what he wanted to do were already fully formed. Like Evans, in his classic *American Photographs*, Frank wished his photographs to speak for themselves, uncaptioned, and let them tell their own stories through the way they were sequenced in a language that was truly the language of photography. Frank had also given up on established ideas of what makes a beautiful picture. In his highly unconventional uses of blur, of tilt, of grainy images, he resembled his contemporary, working in Paris, Ed van der Elsken.

From his hundreds of rolls of film Frank chose just eighty-three images for inclusion in his book, *The Americans*. Well published and well established as he was, he had trouble finding an American publisher for the book. This may have had to do with his insistence on bringing out a book of photographs without accompanying text, but more likely it may have been the disturbing story told by the photographs themselves that made publishers hesitate. The *U.S. Camera Annual 1958* (which came out in 1957) provided a "sneak peek" at a number of the images Frank had made during his Guggenheim travels. Tom Maloney, editor of the annuals, admitted that "Frank's vision of America certainly isn't everyone's picture of the country we live in. This is hardly the inspirational school of photography." Yet he tried to cushion its impact by connecting Frank's work to "the documentary that was so important to photography in the thirties," while he invoked Steichen's authority, saying that Steichen found this work excellent.[13] Walker Evans, in the same issue of *U.S. Camera Annual*, derided "The Family of Man" by contrasting it with Frank's work, calling Frank's work "a far cry from all the woolly, successful 'photo-sentiments' about human familyhood."[14] According to Lili Bezner, Evans championed Frank while undermining contemporary notions of documentary and photojournalism: "Frank becomes (ever-so-gradually) the isolated visionary whose images, Evans predicted, would probably not be accepted by the public."[15] The prediction would not be tested until a few years later, in 1959, when Frank did find a sympathetic American publisher, Grove Press in New York, which published the literary magazine *Evergreen* as well as books by the French literary avant-garde. It may have taken an unusual American publisher, attuned to French cultural sensitivities and their typical mixture of infatuation with American culture and cultural anti-Americanism, to take up Frank's *The Americans*. In fact, the book had been published the year before in France, as *Les Américains*, quickly followed by an Italian edition, *Gli Americani*.

The French edition presented the eighty-three images selected by Frank, accompanied by texts and other materials selected and in a few cases written by the poet, novelist, and man of letters Alain Bosquet. In the Italian edition Bosquet, working with Raffaele Crovi, revised the selection to include Italian authors such as Pavese and Moravia without significantly changing the overall effect. Frank had had no say regarding these texts, and had objected to their use. He thought the criticism of America they contained was propaganda, as opposed to the subtler point of view represented by his photos. The responses to the European editions, embedded as they were in texts that all drew on well-established repertoires of a cultural critique of America, afford a revealing look at how America was perceived in Europe at this particular moment in the Cold War. Bosquet's editorial intervention managed in fact to Europeanize the reading of Frank's photographs, turning them into visual documents to illustrate old European concerns about modernity and mass culture as they were evolving in America and might "spread" (Frank's word in his Guggenheim application) to Europe. As Robert Silberman points out: "America is once again in a familiar double role as the object of both utopian and dystopian concerns."[16] The French and Italian editions made Frank's eye a foreign eye, turning the United States, in an age-old European intellectual game, into Europe's "Other."

For the American edition Frank resumed editorial control and put the book squarely into the ferment of cultural trends and tensions within the United States. He had found Jack Kerouac willing to write an introductory essay. He resolutely stepped back into the world of an American bohemia, with its exhilarating lifestyle of cultural slumming, of a life "on the road" that spanned a continent. While Europeans could only vicariously share such exhilaration, lip-synching the words of "Route 66" and idolizing Kerouac or Ken Kesey, Robert Frank had fully immersed himself in the experience. In the Grove Press edition Frank re-Americanized the context for the reception of his book. Yet did that make his vision less foreign, less un-American, if not anti-American? There may be a tendency now, as part of the larger myth lionizing Frank as the lone, embattled visionary, to exaggerate the rejection of *The Americans* as an anti-American document. To be sure, there were voices making that claim, particularly in two mainstream popular photographic periodicals, *Popular Photography* and *Modern Photography*. Yet, as Bezner insists, the multiple reviews reprinted in *Popular Photography* (July 1960) have been overused as the representative criticism Frank encountered. She convincingly restores balance to this reigning but mistaken recollection of the initial response to *The Americans*.[17] A little facetiously Bezner writes: "Frank might be called the perfect cold war photographer—his work walked the tightrope between social consciousness and political awareness while it remained invested with enough irony to obscure any didactic political clarity. No one named Frank in court, as they had Grossman, for Frank's rebellion was one of spirit and personal alienation from contemporary society."[18]

Frank was not alone as a photographic dissenter. Other photographers in New York presented a less than sanguine view of American life. There was one photographer in particular whose career offers an interesting parallel to Robert Frank's, William Klein. He was an expatriate New Yorker who lived in Paris after the war and studied art on the GI Bill. He then fell into a career as a fashion photographer. In 1954 he spent a relatively brief period back in New York, shooting photographs on the street in an effort to capture the intensity, the energy, the tough-ness of the modern metropolis. His expatriate experience had left him with a left-bank, bohemian affinity, an almost French ambiguity, hover-ing between fascination and aversion. Of the two, fascination may have been the stronger force. Max Kozloff mentions Simone de Beauvoir's reflections on her visit to New York, in 1947. Where she clearly kept her raptures of fascination in check by an authorial, left-wing voice, Klein simply let himself go, as both the insider who knew the place and the outsider he had become. Where Beauvoir always in the end saw through the glittering surface displays and found only the hoax and the hype, Klein could not get enough of either. In his work, as Kozloff puts it, "the deconstructionist meets the absurdist head-on, and the picture wins. He never met an advertisement he didn't like."[19] Klein uses billboards, plas-tered with faces, as subtitles and sound track for a whole culture. He im-plies that New Yorkers live vicariously through their mediascape, even though they are functions of it. There is no background that is not also foreground. In his photographs of people, there is a direct, in-your-face quality of the encounter between photographer and subject, in an almost riotous rapture of seeing. The photographic result is a gritty, lively style that Max Kozloff has described as "slumming with jazzy abandon."[20] Klein assembled his scorching photographs of his hometown in a book that was little recognized by colleagues and was scorned by American publishers at the time. His book, *Life Is Good and Good for You in New York: Trance Witness Revels* (a play on the standard tabloid headline "Chance Witness Reveals"), was published in France in 1956. The title aptly catches the anarchist rapture of someone reveling in the shapes modernity has assumed in New York. The abandon it suggests may have been typical of a bohemian lifestyle in New York and Paris, yet the book's adoption by a Paris publisher may be seen as a proper homecom-ing. Paris at the time was more receptive to Klein's vision of America in the 1950s than were Americans themselves. To them it must have seemed a foreigner's gaze. If there was a lone and scorned visionary among the 1950s photographers who took a distanced and alienating look at Amer-ica it may have been Klein, not Frank.

SEVEN ◉ IMAGINARY AMERICAS IN
EUROPE'S PUBLIC SPACE

WHERE DOES EUROPE END? It is a question of immeasurably greater complexity than the question of where America ends. America as a national entity may extend from sea to shining sea, yet as we also know it projects an image of itself far beyond its national borders. People anywhere in the world can meaningfully connect themselves to inner constructs of what America represents and means to them. With the European Union explosively expanding, now having to digest the presence in its midst of new member states that until the end of the Cold War found themselves under the sway of the Soviet Union, the United States blithely leapfrogs across all the new political borderlines in Europe. Travelers venturing beyond the new eastern border of the European Union find prominent displays of McDonald's golden arches in the Crimea, with a statue of Lenin in the background. They are the further extension of a visual presence of iconic images of American mass culture that featured prominently in European countries west of the Iron Curtain during the Cold War. But such imagery has always been a surface phenomenon overlying the crackled face of Europe and its intricate pattern of fault lines and cultural borderlands. Old Europes have vanished, remembered only by those who once lived in vibrant communities that are no more. In a beautiful book of photographs, *Diaspora: Homelands in Exile,* Frédéric Brenner presents pictures of the survivors of the forty-

Lenin facing McDonald's Golden Arches, Crimea, 2001. Monique van Hoogstraten, photographer. *Private collection.*

five thousand Jews who had made Salonika, in Greece, virtually a Jewish city.[1] In 1943 they were sent to Auschwitz, where more than 90 percent of them were murdered. Until the beginning of the past century Salonika had been a kind of Sephardi republic: cosmopolitan, Europeanized, linked with London, Vienna, Belgrade, and Istanbul by the Orient Express. As a Jewish city-state it had lasted from the expulsion of the Jews from Spain in 1492 to the Greco-Turkish treaty of 1923, when 100,000 Greeks from Anatolia and Asia Minor were settled there by the government in an attempt to hellenize it and end the dominant role of the Jewish majority. German fascism finished it off altogether.

In one of Brenner's photographs of the Jewish diaspora, four men form a remnant of what was once the largest Jewish community in the whole of the Orient. Three are on the right of the picture, one on the left. Three fists, two tattooed with their concentration camp number, grip a wooden post. The man to the left of the post holds his hand, palm open, against his face, his own tattoo also visible. Brenner has asked a number of intellectuals, academics, poets, and novelists to write short

The Marlboro Man in the Crimea, 2001. Monique van Hoogstraten, photographer.
Private collection.

essays on a selection of the photographs in his book. No one has much
trouble describing the three men on the right. As Sidra Dekoven
Ezrahi, a professor of comparative literature at the Hebrew University,
Jerusalem, writes: "the face of defiance, vengeance, the will to power . . .
'Never again!' shout these grim voiceless faces and those fisted hands."

But over the man on the left there is great confusion. Are we looking at the binary opposite of the other three—suffering versus vengeance—"sorrow, humility and compassion," as Ezrahi writes? Or can one detect a "twinkle in the eye and the ever so slight hint of a tender smile," as the poet Ammiel Alcalay suggests? I couldn't say. In any case, this photograph as well as the others, gathered in a twenty-five-year journey by the photographer, all testify to the tragedy of European history. Many Europes, many vibrant communities, have come to an end, leaving hardly a trace other than in the memory of scattered survivors. This suggests one answer to the question of where Europe ends. Many Europes have ended many times over, because of genocide, population transfers, ethnic cleansing, and internecine war. As in the movement of tectonic plates, historic forms of Europe have submerged, melted into oblivion.

But Europe ends in different ways as well. Looked at in a certain way, the map of Europe offers a mosaic of borderlands, of invisible lines separating communities from each other. Regional communities, historically rooted, see their cohesion threatened by restless migration movements or more generally by the wider horizons brought by modernization and globalization. Diasporic communities, of Turks, Moroccans, Algerians, live among members of their host societies, on the margin, in cultural interstices, yet with a protocosmopolitan sense of the larger European space that they now inhabit, straddling national borders. Certain established Europes, as defined by those sharing a sense of cultural commonality, draw lines to include or exclude neighbors. They are all lines where certain Europes end and rub shoulders with new Europes struggling to emerge.

As I argued before, overlying all this is the idea at least of a larger Europe, offering a framework for meaningful identification to all denizens of the new, emerging Europe. It is a dream more than a reality at the moment. In a stunning collection of photographs, on show in the summer of 2004 in the Kunsthal in Rotterdam, Dutch photographer Nicole Segers displayed pictures taken along the new eastern border of the European Union, from Finland all the way down to Bulgaria. They mostly are bleak pictures of people left astray by the turmoil of political change since the end of the Cold War. Segers, the photographer, was accompanied by a journalist friend, Irene van der Linde, who interviewed many of the people who found themselves without bearings. Many are now citizens of the European Union. In one conversation, a Bulgarian fisherman says: "You feel it if you love someone and you feel it if someone loves you." The fisherman takes a pause, like an actor on stage. Everyone sits in silence. "In the case of Europe, I feel nothing." After these words, all the fishermen at the table raise their glass. "Nazdrave," they toast. "Let us drink to this." "Welcome to the end of Europe."[2]

This end of Europe, where people do not have any feelings about the larger political community that now defines their citizenship, is to be found not only at the extreme eastern border of the Union. People all across Europe feel no meaningful affiliation with the "New Europe" and are in anguished search for more meaningful frameworks to define their citizenship. In that sense there are many "liminal Europes," situations where Europe dims into irrelevance as if it reaches its far borders. There are as yet few overarching emblems helping people to conceive of the larger Europe. There are no potent iconic images in the way that America has projected them onto the European canvas. In what follows I propose to contrast these two situations, the crackled pattern of liminal Europes and the presence across Europe of imaginary Americas.

Needed: An Archeology of Europe as Remembered Space

In my education as a European—a haphazard trajectory at best, never consistently set out or pursued—I remember one formative moment. I had the good fortune, as an undergraduate in political science, to find a book on the required reading list—Edward Atiyah's *The Arabs*[3]—that shook my established views of the history of Western civilization. I had had the privilege before to attend an old-style Dutch gymnasium and had read some of the classics from antiquity, such as Homer in Greek or Virgil in Latin, in addition to some of the great works in four modern languages, German, French, English, and of course Dutch. It had left me with a mistaken sense of unilinear evolution from Greek and Roman times to modern European civilization. Thus I had an etymological sense of the modern languages at my command, including those of Germanic origin, as resonant with ancient Greek and Latin. I saw Goethe, Shakespeare, and Racine as inspired by the masters of antiquity. Words like Renaissance and Enlightenment only confirmed my reading of Western civilization as repeatedly reinvigorating itself by returning to its intellectual and artistic origins. Everything in my high school education had worked to instill in me this sense of history as a transformational process, continuing in one unbroken line, for all its inner hybridity and the admixtures from other sources. My sense and that of many others was the unreflected latter-day version of the old myth of the Westward Course of Empire and Civilization or, as it was known in the days when Europe's common language was still Latin, the *Translatio Studii et Imperii*. This myth was taken up by Bishop Berkeley in the eighteenth century and projected onto the canvas of America; his poem would be eagerly adopted by Americans in the nineteenth century as one of the historical justifications for their westward expansion in what they saw as their manifest destiny.[4] From Virgil to Berkeley there was this sense of an unbroken line of Western civilization evolving over time, while it traveled ever farther westward. Nothing had prepared me for my reading of Atiyah's book.

He presents Arab civilization, at the time of its greatest flowering, not as something out there, beyond the self-enclosed sphere of a European world immersed in its own process of civilization, but as critically linked to it, in dialogue, in cultural encounters and clashes, nurturing and further enriching a classical heritage, appropriating it before Europeans claimed it as exclusively theirs. Not only does Atiyah interweave the story of Arab civilization with that of European civilization, offering a larger cosmopolitan perspective; he also explodes current conceptual habits that see Arabs as a homogeneous "Them" versus an equally homogeneous "Us." At the time of its greatest geographical reach the Arab empire held a population of immense variety, religiously, ethnically, and linguistically, yet freely intermingling, and fully partaking of the intellectual and cultural ferment in its urban centers. Atiyah forever changed my mental map of the history of what we now call Western civilization, of its locale as much as of its agency. Europe as an organizing idea, conflating a geological landmass with the stage on which Western civilization unfolded, would henceforth be a blur rather than offer a clear focus.

Much the same story could be told about the Ottoman Empire, successor to the Arab era of cultural and political predominance. It was centered in one of the great European cities, which under the name of Constantinople had for a thousand years been a cultural haven in the history of Christendom, in addition to being a cosmopolitan crossroads. The Ottomans, confusingly and tellingly, invaded Constantinople from Europe, entering the city through its west gate, and renamed it Istanbul. They appropriated its rich cultural landscape rather than razing it, in marked contrast to the pillage and desecration of a then Orthodox Christian Constantinople at the hands of Frankish crusaders in 1204. Under the Ottomans Christian iconography was plastered over, not iconoclastically smashed to pieces. In the cultural sedimentation of history a new layer was added, like a new coat of paint. In cultural syncretism mosques were built emulating the grand structure of the Aya Sophia. Again, artisans, artists, and intellectuals from inside the realm as well as from outside, in fact from all over the larger Mediterranean world, flocked there to contribute to Ottoman civilization. Ironically, with the Ataturk turn toward a radical Western secularism and nationalism, seeking to westernize Turkish society following the breakup of the Ottoman Empire, the Aya Sophia was decommissioned as a mosque and restored to its former Christian symbolism. Frescoes and mosaics have been uncovered, and they now sit alongside the later Muslim iconography honoring Mahomet and the first four caliphs. It is a lasting memento to the history of related, though rival, civilizations washing across each other, in an ongoing ebb and flow.

As happens so often, rivals locked in combat in the end turn out to resemble each other. Within the Christian world the mirror image of the two great Muslim empires is without a doubt the Austro-Hungarian Empire, deriving its cultural sense of itself from its longtime struggle against the expansionist Ottomans as its cultural Other. Yet the resemblance is striking in terms of the multiethnic cultural vibrancy, centered in the Austrian case on its seat of empire, Vienna. Nor was the dividing line ever very neat in religious terms. Muslims and Christians lived alongside each other on either side of the line, although tolerance of religious diversity may have been greater under the Ottomans. If tolerance is a virtue claimed on behalf of European civilization, which of the two empires then was more European?

The question is meant to be more than merely flippant. In Christianity's defense against two successful Muslim empires, there was always an exclusionist reading of its cause, a driving sense of religious purity. It fired the fervor of the Crusades; it was behind the Spanish *riconquista,* as much as it inspired later religious wars on European soil. Compared with the religious live-and-let-live attitude in the Muslim empires, what a sorry sight it is to see the successful Christian reconquest of the Iberian Peninsula seamlessly blend into the expulsion of the Jews. Nor were the Spaniards alone in this endeavor. In a letter to the French king the Dutch humanist Erasmus, trying to flatter him, complimented him on making France free of Jews. Elsewhere as well anti-Semitism served the purpose of creating the necessary Other for cementing cultural homogeneity, around versions of Christianity first, and notions of the nation later. Slowly but surely much of Europe began to harden around lines of social and cultural exclusivism. Alien communities were hounded out, their places of worship demolished, their graveyards plowed under.

Amazingly, after all these years, Europeans still could not believe their eyes when this same logic of ethnic cleansing attended the breakup of yet another multiethnic state on European soil, Yugoslavia. It was the latest frantic attempt at cleansing from the map of Europe traces reminiscent of earlier forms of communal and cultural life. Photographs and television footage of Sarajevo, showing a multiethnic and cosmopolitan place in the grand Austro-Hungarian tradition being shelled by surrounding Serb artillery, left European viewers speechless and powerless. Pictures of concentration camps, showing emaciated inmates clutching the fence that held them captive, evoked instant associations with Nazi atrocities that Europeans might have hoped were forever in the past. The pictures, and the associations they called forth, triggered collective memories and provided a ready historical context for the interpretation of what was going on in Bosnia. Yet it took unconscionably long for the West actively to intervene. Impotent anger was the first response. As Barbie Zelizer points out in this context, there is a paradox in this conflation of atrocities remembered and atrocities recently perpetrated. "The insistence on remembering earlier atrocities may not necessarily promote active responses to new instances of brutality. [I have] argued that the opposite, in fact, may be true: we may remember earlier atrocities so as to forget the contemporary ones."[5] I am not sure whether I agree with her last point. As I remember it, it was precisely the fact that associations with Nazi atrocities were triggered that gave contemporary witnesses a sense of the enormity of what was going on, and created a large popular pressure in Europe and the United States not to stand by but to intercede and stop the brutality. Other, more shameful memories came back. After all, nothing had been done during World War II to stop or hinder the Holocaust while it was going on. The photographs that bore ample witness to the atrocities that had taken place were all taken after the fact. Now, in Bosnia, photographs showed atrocities as they were going on. Now was the time to act. In the end, "cleansing" was brought to a halt before it had a chance to run its full dismal course.

The Balkan tragedies of the 1990s may have shown demonic dimensions, which may make them seem to stand apart as a throwback to a past we mistakenly thought we had forever put behind us; yet the sorting out of European populations along lines of ethnic and cultural purity proceeds apace across the map of Europe, with greater or lesser violence. It ranges from the Basque country, Ulster, and Corsica all the way to the successor states of the former Soviet empire. There is much unfinished business on the agenda of cultural purity and homogeneity.

The logic inherent in all this may be of a European vintage, centering for the last two centuries on the purity of the nation or of subnational entities such as cultural regions. But it has proved contagious. Thus, in the course of a mere one hundred years following the breakup of the Ottoman Empire, Turkey as one of its successor nation-states lost much of its cosmopolitan diversity, through the forced expulsion of Greeks, whose settlement in fact predated the advent of the Turks on the peninsula, or through the voluntary emigration of people who had given Istanbul its cosmopolitan flavor. Internal migration from the countryside in Anatolia to the industrial labor market of Istanbul exploded its population while making it, demographically and culturally speaking, ever more Asian (its population at the turn of the century was about 25–30 percent Kurdish). As a result, Turkey's most European city has seen its westernized Turkish bourgeoisie and its international community become an ever smaller minority.

Given this reordering of the map of Europe over the last centuries, this willful erasing of remnants and markers of earlier social arrangements, it is small wonder that most people living in Europe see the current map as the natural one. To them, this is how things are and how they have always been. As I mentioned before, I had to rid myself as a student of this habit of mind when reading a book about Arab civilization. The book, for me, served the purpose of an archeological exercise in recovering older memories of European space, suppressed and willfully forgotten, yet of great value for current debates concerning what Europe is and is not. High school textbooks across Europe would need to be rewritten, with a view to unsettling the pernicious presentism of people's ideas about Europe. This ideal new textbook would have to offer a tour across European space, forgetting about borders and current lines on the map and turning it into one big memory space, a *lieu de mémoire*, the sort of space as it emerges from W. G. Sebald's journeys across time and space, stumbling upon triggers of memory, bringing back voices long gone silent, shimmering faces emerging from mists before being enveloped by them once again. We need to construct Europe as its own underworld, with ghosts wandering about, demanding to be heard. We need museums, of Jewish history, of colonial history, of regional history, of maps of past Europes, smaller than its landmass or extending far beyond it, museums of population movements, forced or voluntary, of diasporic communities like people of Turkish descent in Germany and the Netherlands finding a new sense of self. We need film and photographs, documenting Europes long since vanished. We need interviews with people who now live where others lived before them, in the ruthless succession of populations across the map of Europe, asking them what, if anything, they remember. We need to look at Europe from its liminal points, following a perimeter of contested terrain. And more often than not the liminal points are inside Europe, rather than at its perimeter, as gatekeeping devices for the cultural and civic exclusion of those considered outsiders. We need a map of Europe showing only cultural islands, its pure cultural regions as people see them, and then showing what larger cultural currents wash across these outposts of insulation. We need to turn present-day Europeans into a new audience beholding the pageant of earlier Europes that they should but often do not remember.

These would all be necessary exercises in what I called the archeology of remembered space. Yet we need not recover only the past through uncovering Europe's layered history. Layers are being added right before our eyes, affecting, as they should and for millions actually do, the collective sense of European space, or rather of the many Europes as people now construct them in the wake of the Cold War. In films and writing many creative minds have set out to explore the debris left by the receding tide of Soviet power.

At the end of Anne Applebaum's journey described in *Between East and West: Across the Borderlands of Europe*, from Kaliningrad on the Baltic through Lithuania, Belarus, Ukraine, Bukovina, Moldova, and Transnistria to Odessa, she crosses the Black Sea, arriving in the Bosphorus at dawn, and is struck by the color, energy, and prosperity after months of an ex-socialist drabness of brown and gray: "Ahead of us gleamed the minarets of Istanbul. I was back in the West."[6] As Moray McGowan astutely comments, this exemplifies unusually clearly how meaning and identity are relative and constituted through oppositions.[7] Istanbul is usually invoked in Western discourse as a bridge between East and West or as a quintessentially Oriental city. But Applebaum, by viewing it as part of a bright, affluent West in contrast to a physically drab and psychologically depressed ex-communist East, locates it, surely with conscious irony, within another, familiar, but very different polarity, that of the Cold War. In Cold War terms, Turkey, NATO's key southeastern flank, belonged to "Europe" as defined by Western powers. Walter Hallstein had, as president of the European Commission at the time of Turkey's Treaty of Association in 1964, declared emphatically that "Turkey is part of Europe."[8] This same Hallstein had given his name, as McGowan reminds us,[9] to the West German "Doctrine" of 1955, which, in a microcosm of Western Cold War positions, sought to isolate the German Democratic Republic (GDR) by threatening to sever relations with any third state that recognized it. In certain circumstances, then, Turkey was more Western, more "European," than East Germany.

Switching to film, there is a masterpiece by the young Swedish director Lukas Moodysson titled *Lilya 4-ever*, a bleak and devastatingly powerful study of Lilya, a poverty-stricken teenage girl abandoned in a crumbling Russian town in an unspecified Baltic state. The girl is left behind when her mother leaves, apparently for the United States, with a man she has met through a dating agency. In her wretchedness Lilya finds a friend in a lonely eleven-year-old boy, Volodya, but then duplicates her mother's betrayal when she meets a smooth-talking young guy who says he can take her away to Sweden, like "America" another beckoning escape from her pauperized and hopeless life. As it turns out, Sweden offers captivity and slavery rather than liberation. Visually, the director shows us a Sweden that is not all that different from the wasteland of the former Soviet empire. Blocks of apartment high-rises may be in a better state of repair, but otherwise look as grim and forbidding as anything in the East. On arriving in Sweden, Lilya finds that the promised job was a trick. Imprisoned and forced into prostitution, the girl is repeatedly raped, day after day after day, in ways that Moodysson pitilessly shows us from her perspective. Forced prostitution is shown as a horrible reality, one that links the impoverished post-Soviet states and the sex industry in the moneyed West.

If this film conflates "Europe" and "America" as paradises of freedom and riches, the connection comes out more strongly in a film by Italian director Gianni Amelio, *L'America*. It depicts another post-Communist state, Albania, as a place of unspeakable horror, where anarchy, brutality, and corruption are rampant. The film offers a frightening view of a world devoid of the least trace of civil protection as we value it in the West, a world where every civil institution has collapsed. The final images of escape from this nightmarish landscape by ship present it in the light of a crossing to "America," although the ship in fact only crosses the Adriatic to Italy. Yet the images are visually reminiscent of ships entering New York harbor, with the steerage passengers out en masse to behold the land of promise.

But we need not enter the fringe of the former Soviet empire to get a glimpse of the threats to civil life in Europe. A film by Spanish director Helena Taberna, *Yoyes*, takes a sobering look at the Leninism and terrorism that characterize the movement for Basque national emancipation (ETA). Although the movement's early appeal lay in its use of a language of cultural rights and ethnic self-determination, finding its roots in the larger liberationist enthusiasms of the 1960s, the means it used in pursuit of its goals were a travesty of the rules of the democratic game. Since democracy came to Spain, ETA has lived a life of denial of its changed environment and has withdrawn into the conspiratorial worldview of a small band of hardened activists. The film tells the true story of a woman member of ETA, a participant in many of its violent actions, who after a period of exile in Paris wants to return to the Basque country and resume a normal civilian life. In retaliation for her defection and denunciation of ETA's totalitarianism, ETA activists execute her in cold blood. When she takes a walk with friends, someone calls her by her name; she turns around and is shot straight in the face. It took courage to make the film in the Basque country, given the climate of fear and intimidation that effectively silences the voices of dissent and obscures the plurality of views among the Basque population. A film like *Yoyes*, which allows its audience to widen its view and to look across Europe's borders, deserves a far wider distribution than *Yoyes* actually got. If one of Europe's problems is the creation of truly

European audiences, Europe's film and television industries need all the support they can get for the visual representation of Europe's many faces for European audiences.

One further contemporary film, *Russian Arc* by the Russian director Alexander Sokurrow, is an example of such a transnational collaborative effort, in terms of its financing and distribution. Ironically, it may have had a greater *succes d'estime* in the United States than in Europe. As almost a cult film it has run for months in art houses in New York and other big cities in the United States. Although acclaimed by the European press, its public exposure in Europe does not compare with that in the United States.[10] The film takes us back to the archeology of Europe as remembered space. Loosely based on Astolphe de Custine's classic *La Russie en 1839*, it brings the French nobleman back to life as a ghost from the nineteenth century wandering about the premises of the Saint Petersburg Hermitage, but wandering through time as well. At times rooms are filled with present-day Russians, whom the Frenchman engages in conversation, on occasion scolding them for their lack of historical appreciation of paintings that collectively represent European culture. At other moments, in other rooms, we are taken back in time to the days of Catherine the Great, or of the last czar shown in the midst of his family on the eve of the Revolution. The final scenes are of a ball in the main ballroom, with the upper crust dancing to music by Glinka, a Russian composer of music in a Western vein. With apparent gusto Valery Gergiev, a cosmopolitan star in the world of music, conducts the costumed orchestra. Then, in ominous foreboding of an era coming to its end, we see the hundreds of guests descending the stairs, in a seemingly endless procession. The final shot takes our gaze outside the building, through an open door, into a bleak and nebulous night, as a stark reminder of the dark times ahead, an era in which Russia's infatuation with a bourgeois Europe would be only a distant memory. The film is one astounding, uninterrupted take. The director turns his camera into yet another character in the film, invisible to all, except the French nobleman. They engage in conversation, with the Frenchman going through raptures at the European culture on display, or mimicked in the lavish architecture and interior design of the Hermitage. He tends to disparage Russian culture. It makes his skin itch. Yet in the end he joins the dance, satisfied with the Russian version of the good life in Europe. When all the others leave, he refuses to go along. He would rather continue his ghostly existence as a perennial nostalgic. He takes a little bow to his camera friend and says: "Good-bye, Europe."

Custine's *La Russie en 1839* came out at about the same time as the classic work of another French nobleman, Alexis de Tocqueville's *De la démocratie en Amérique*. Custine had measured Russia by the standards of European high taste and high culture; Tocqueville had gone to America to try to fathom what democracy in America, as the wave of a future coming to Europe, would mean for Europe's cultural landscape. Tocqueville's view was typically ambivalent. He marveled at the vitality of democratic life in the American republic. Aware of the old wisdoms concerning the life cycle of republics, from early vigor to decline and on to eventual demise, he wondered about the secrets of the apparent stability of America's republic. His insights crucially concerned the forms of social, or "associative," life in America rather than the intricacy of its constitutional apparatus. Its political stability was anchored in its social pluralism. Tocqueville was among the first to explore "civil society," the social sphere beyond the reach of government control or surveillance, and critically dependent on democratic freedoms. Only they allowed the citizenry to be the agent of its manifold associative activities, ranging from political parties to churches, schools, and the many other forms of group activities in pursuit of collective interests.

If Tocqueville's grasp of the voluntarism that was characteristic of democratic life made him one of the fathers of modern sociology, his exploration of the impact of mass democracy on culture made him a precursor in a long line of critics of mass culture. Here his views are much more sobering. They held out a warning to Europeans with their more aristocratic views of taste hierarchies and the role of cultural elites. Tocqueville was keenly aware of the leveling effects of cultural production under democratic conditions, aiming as it did at the lowest common denominator of public taste rather than catering to the tastes of social elites. Culture followed the dictates of majority conformism rather than the intricate games of cultural distinction characteristic of Europe's stratified societies. Both his views of the self-sustaining forces of democracy in America and his views of cultural life under democratic conditions were informed by his sense that what he had observed in America was a prefiguration of Europe's future. If Custine's book explored European culture as it was appropriated on its eastern frontier, Tocqueville foresaw the advent of mass society as a force undermining European culture from within. As it happened, much of this erosion would be seen by later culture critics not as indigenous but as a process of Europeans appropriating forms of American mass culture. If Bishop Berkeley had seen a westward course of empire and civilization, the twentieth century, also known as the American century, would see a reverse course. The empire, once it had reached American shores, would now strike back, Americanizing Europe in its turn.

Many have been the discussions in Europe as to what exactly it was that America, seen as the harbinger of Europe's future, held in store. Germany had its *Amerikanismus* debate in the 1920s; France for over two centuries looked on in fascination and trepidation as modernity in its American guise unfolded. Intellectuals in many other countries contributed their views as they observed the American scene.[11] Many traveled there and reported back to their various home audiences; others stayed home trying to fathom the forms of reception and appropriation of the American model, in culture, in economics, and in politics. More often than not the form of these critical exchanges was one of triangulation. Parties engaged in debate on how to structure the future in Europe's various nation-states used America as a reference point to define their positions, either rejecting the American model or promoting it for adoption. I have written extensively on these processes of triangulation.[12] In the following I propose to take a different approach. I will look at the presence of iconographic representations of America across Europe, exploring the ways in which they may have affected the sense of European space among Europeans.

American Iconography in Europe's Public Space

I must have been twelve or thirteen, in the early 1950s, when in my home town of Haarlem in the Netherlands I stood enthralled by a huge picture along the entire rear wall of a garage. As I remember it now, it was my first trancelike transportation into a world that was unlike anything I had known so far. I stood outside on the sidewalk looking in. Not surprisingly, given the fact that this garage sold American cars, the picture on the wall was of a 1950s American car shown in its full iconographic force as a carrier of dreams rather than as a mere means of transportation. Cars in general, let alone their gigantic American versions, were a distant dream to most Dutch people at the time. Yet what held my gaze was not so much the car as the image of a boy, younger than I was at the time, who came rushing from behind the car, his motion stopped, his contagious joy continuing. He wore sneakers, blue jeans rolled up at the ankles, a T-shirt. His hairdo was different from that of any of my friends, and so was his facial expression. Come to think of it, there must have been a ball. The boy's rush must have been like the exhilarating dash across a football field or a basketball court, surging ahead of others. The very body language, although frozen into a still picture, seemed to speak of a boisterous freedom. Everything about the boy radiated signals from a distant but enticing world.

This may have been my first confrontation with a wide-screen display of the good life in America, of its energy, its exhilaration, its typical pursuits and satisfactions. As I now think back on the moment, I am aware that my distant exposure to America's dreamscape was not unlike an astronomer's, catching light emitted aeons ago by distant stars. Metaphorically speaking, America was aeons away from Europe at the time, feverishly engaged as it was in the construction of the consumers' republic and the pursuit of happiness that this incited. Beholding a picture of America in a garage in Haarlem, I was exposed to a representation of life in America in a rare reflection of public imagery that in America had become ubiquitous. Nor was such imagery all that recent there. Even at the depth of the Great Depression the National Association of Manufacturers (N.A.M.), in typical boosterism, had pasted similar images across the nation, advertising "The American Way" in displays of happy families riding in their cars. Much of the jarring dissonance between these public displays and the miseries of collective life in 1930s America still applied to Europe in the early 1950s. Those were still lean years. In Haarlem I stood beholding an image that had no visual referent in real life anywhere in Europe. Yet the image may have been equally seductive for Europeans as for Americans. Consumerism may have been a distant dream in postwar Europe, yet it was eagerly anticipated as Europeans were exposed to its American version, through advertising, photojournalism, and Hollywood films.

Now, as images of America's culture of consumption began to fill Europe's public space, they exposed Europeans to views of the good life that Americans themselves were exposed to. To that extent they may have Americanized European dreams and longings. But isn't there also a way we might argue that Europe's exposure to American imagery may have worked to Europeanize Europe at the same time? There are several ways of going about answering this question. It has been said in jest that the only culture that Europeans had in common in the later twentieth century was American culture. Their exposure to forms of American mass culture transcended national borders in ways that no national varieties were ever able to rival. True, there was the occasional Italian or German hit song running up the charts in other European countries. There were still audiences across Europe for films made in one or another European country. There were the 1960s, when England contributed to international youth culture in areas such as music and fashion, often giving its own characteristic twist to the American mass culture that had reached England in the years before. But the one continuing line throughout the latter half of the twentieth century was of an exposure of European publics to American mass culture.

The points of exposure were not necessarily only in public space. Much of the consumption of American mass culture took place in private settings when people watched television in their living rooms, or Hollywood movies in the quasi-private space of the darkened movie theater. American popular music reached them via the radio or on records and once again made for a formation of audiences assembling in private places, such as homes or dance clubs. This private, or peer-group, consumption of American mass culture does not mean that larger virtual audiences did not emerge across Europe. Far from it. Shared repertoires, shared tastes, and shared cultural memories formed that would make for quick and easy cultural exchange across national borders among Europe's younger generations. They could more readily compare notes on shared cultural preferences by using American examples than by using varieties of mass culture produced in their own national settings.

Yet this is not what I have in mind to explore here. There is an area, properly called public space, outside private homes, outside gathering places for cultural consumption, that has served across Europe as a site of exposure to American mass culture. Much as it is true that forms of American mass culture, transmitted via the entertainment industry, travel under commercial auspices—are always economic commodities in addition to being cultural goods, to be sold before they are consumed—public space is the area where American mass culture has most openly advertised itself, creating the demand if not the desire for its consumption. In public space, including the press, we find the film posters advertising the latest Hollywood movies, or the dreamlike representations of an America where people smoke certain cigarettes, buy certain cars, cosmetics, clothes. They are literally advertisements, creating economic demand, while conveying imaginary Americas at the same time. They have thus contributed to a European repertoire of an invented America, as a realm for reverie, filled with iconic heroes, setting standards of physical beauty, of taste, of proper behavior. If Europe to a certain extent has become "other-directed," much like America itself under the impact of its own commercial culture, Europe's significant Other became America, as commercially constructed through advertising.

If we may conceive of this redirection of Europe's gaze toward America as a sign of Europe's Americanization, it means an appropriation of American standards and tastes in addition to whatever cultural habits were already in place to direct people's individual quest for identity. Americanization is never a simple zero-sum game where people trade in their European clothes for every pair of blue jeans they acquire. It is more a matter of cultural syncretism, of an interweaving of bits of American culture into European cultural habits, where every borrowing of American cultural ingredients creatively changes their meaning and context. Certainly, Europe's cultural landscape has changed, but never in ways that would lead visiting Americans to mistake Europe for a simple replica of their own culture.

My larger point, though, is to pursue a paradox. Henry James at one point astutely perceived that it is for Americans rather than Europeans to conceive of Europe as a whole, and to transcend Europe's patterns of cultural particularism. He meant to conceive of it as one cultural canvas on a scale commensurate with that of America as one large continental culture. His aphoristic insight certainly highlights a recurring rationale in the way that Americans have approached Europe, whether they are businessmen seeing Europe as one large market for their products or post–World War II politicians pursuing a vision of European cooperation transcending Europe's divisive nationalisms. If we may rephrase James's remark as referring to an inclination of Americans to project their mental scale of thought onto the map of Europe, that inclination in its own right may have had a cultural impact in Europe as an eye-opening revision of their mental compass, inspiring a literal re-vision.

Whatever the precise message, the fact that American advertising appeared across European countries exposed traveling Europeans to commercial communication proceeding across national borders, addressing Europeans wherever they lived. More specifically, though, there is a genre of advertising that precisely confronts Europeans with the fantasy image of America as one large, open space. If all American advertising conjures up fantasy versions of life in America, the particular fantasy of America as unbounded space, free of the confining boundaries set by European cultures to dreams of individual freedom, may well have activated the dream of a Europe as wide and open as America. The particular genre of advertising I am thinking of finds its perfect illustration in the myth of Marlboro Country and the Marlboro Man. The idea of tying the image of this particular brand of cigarette to the mythical lure of the American West goes back to the early 1960s, and it inspired an advertising iconography that kept its appeal until the present day (at least in those countries that have not banned cigarette advertising). Over time the photographic representation of the imaginary space of Marlboro Country expanded in size, filling Europe's public space with wide-screen images of western landscapes, lit by a setting sun, with rock formations glowing in deep red color, with horses descending to their watering hole, and rugged-faced cowboys lighting up after the day's work had been done. This was a space for fantasy to roam, offering the transient escape into dreams of unbounded freedom, of being one's own free agent. It was hard not to see these images. They were often obtrusively placed, hanging over the crowds in railway stations, or adding gorgeous color to some of Europe's gray public squares. I remember one prominently placed to the left of the steps leading up to Budapest's great, gray Museum of Art. The show opened right there. One couldn't miss it.

The formula was widely imitated. Other cigarette brands came up with their own variations on the theme, using different iconography, showing young couples in leisure-time pursuits, or showing a jet-set lifestyle that one might vicarously share for the time it took to smoke a cigarette. In post–Cold War Poland a roadside poster showed a young couple radiating joy, its text inviting the audience "to have a taste of freedom." The advertisement was for an American cigarette. But European cigarette makers as well adopted the approach, as in the French Gauloises campaign, using Parisian settings. The attractive, young males in the photographs have a casual informality about them, with jackets flung over their shoulders or their feet up on the table of a roadside terrace,

that is vaguely resonant of American styles of public behavior. The overall impression is summarily captured in the advertisements' affirmative
statement: "La liberté, toujours." Peter Stuyvesant cigarettes in the Netherlands used a more postmodern collage technique for conveying a similar message. Its ads reduced the explicit markers of European dreams of
America as open space, so central to the Marlboro approach, to mere
echoes to trigger the same repertoire of fantasies. They showed young
couples in the gathering places of an international leisure class, captioned in each case by the name of a hotel in Miami Beach, San Francisco, or other such rendezvous places. The central slogan, giving meaning to the jumble of text and visuals, reads: "There are no borders." The
advertising campaign was set up by a Dutch advertising agency as further testimony to the adoption by Europeans of American dreams and
messages of unbounded space. The use of English in a campaign addressing a Dutch audience has become increasingly common, and is intended to give an international flavor to the message. Indeed, there are
no borders.

In fact the commodified lure of open space has by now become so familiar that advertisers have begun to give an ironic twist to their messages implying a wink to an audience of initiates. One example of this
use of irony is a commercial for an Italian travel agency calling itself
Marlboro Country Travels. Playing on the escapism of much modern
tourism, where you have to lose yourself in the hope of finding yourself,
it arranges travel to the United States while casting the destination in
the image of Marlboro Country's fictional space. A large color photograph, actually a montage, shows a 1950s gas pump, a nostalgic reminder
of the romanticism of Route 66 ("Get your kicks on Route 66"), of Jack
Kerouac's *On the Road,* or of the exhilaration of road movies. As a backdrop the photograph offers a view of the American West, with a little
cloud of dust at its center trailing a diminutive SUV rolling off into the
distance. The central slogan says: "Fai il vuoto" (Go for the void). It plays
on the standard request at gas stations to "fill 'er up" (Fai il pieno). It
beautifully captures the desire of modern travelers to empty themselves
of their concerns and preoccupations, to leave all their worries behind
and take off into empty space.

A similar punning approach to advertising can be found all over Europe's public space nowadays. Freedom still is the central idea in these
games, although it is given many ironic twists. There was a poster for

Marlboro Country travels—Italian advertisement.

Levi's 508 jeans pasted all over the Netherlands in the mid-1990s. The photograph shows a male torso, naked from the neck down to the pair of blue jeans. The iconography has a high degree of intertextuality, at least to an audience steeped in American mass culture. It is reminiscent of Bruce Springsteen's cover for his album *Born in the USA,* or of Andy Warhol's cover design for the Rolling Stones album *Sticky Fingers.* Again, the poster uses a collage technique, offering a jumble of visual and textual ingredients. Surprisingly, given that this is an advertisement designed by a Dutch agency, in the lower left-hand corner we see a variation on Roosevelt's famous four freedoms. The first two sound pretty Rooseveltian, evoking the freedoms of speech and expression, followed by the freedom of choice (not among Roosevelt's foursome, and sitting ambivalently astride the freedom of choice of people seen either as political citizens or as individual consumers). In fourth place, following the words "Levi's 508" in boldface, is the freedom of movement. Again there is the political ring, expressive of a political longing that many in Eastern Europe may have felt during the years of the Cold War. Yet a pun is intended. The freedom of movement in this context is meant to refer to the greater movement offered by the baggier cut of the 508, a point

Dutch poster for Levi's 508.

visually illustrated by the unmistakable bulge of a male member in full erection, touched casually at the tip by the right hand of its master.

The list of further examples is endless. Advertising across Europe's public space has assumed common forms of address, common routines, and common themes (with many variations). Originating in America, it has now been appropriated by European advertising agencies and may be put in the service of American as well as European products. That in itself is a sign of a transnational integration of Europe's public space. But as I suggested before, the point of many of the stories that advertisements tell refers precisely to space, to openness, to a dreamscape transcending Europe's checkered map. An international commercial culture has laid itself across public space in Europe, using an international language, often literally in snippets of English, and instilling cravings and desires now shared internationally. Has all this gone on without voices of protest and resistance rising in these same public spaces?

In fact there have been many instances of such contestation, turning Europe's public space into yet another showcase of liminal Europes. Right at the heart of Europe, in its public space, we can see battle lines running as so many indications of groups pitting themselves against forces of globalization and their appropriation. If appropriation, however playfully and creatively done, is a form of acceptance, we can see many signs of rejection at the same time. On a highway outside Warsaw I saw a poster for ladies' lingerie, using the familiar techniques of drawing the spectator's gaze. It used the female body, shown here from the back, in reference (if not deference) to international ideals of female beauty. If such pictures are apt to draw the male gaze, they do so indirectly, through the male gaze as internalized by women. This is what they would like to look like in the eyes of men. The poster further used the appeal of English. The brand of lingerie was called "Italian Fashion," throwing in the appeal of Italian fashion design for good measure. But evidently, such public display of the female body was not to everyone's taste in Poland. Someone had gotten out his or her spray can to write the Polish word *Dosh* (meaning "Enough" or "Stop it") across the poster. If a he, he may have been a devout Catholic protesting against the desecration of public space; if a she, she may have been a feminist objecting to the commodification of the female body. In another instance, in the northern Italian city of Turin, my gaze was drawn to the base of an equestrian statue. On all four sides, another spray-can artist had left these public messages: "McDonald bastardi," "Boycotta Mc-Donald," and more such. If the square had been turned into a liminal Europe, with Europeans putting up resistance to what they saw as foreign encroachments, it had happened in a rather ironic if not self-defeating way. The point of the protest may have been to rise in defense of the European cultural heritage, but the protester did not shrink from turning one emblem of that heritage, an equestrian statue, into a mere blackboard for messages, desecrating what the protest meant to elevate.

In Europe's lasting encounter with American mass culture, many have been the voices expressing a concern about its negative impact. Cultural guardians in Europe saw European standards of taste and cultural appreciation eroded by an American way with culture that aimed at a mass market, elevating the lowest common denominator of mass preferences to the main vector of cultural production. This history of cultural anti-Americanism in Europe has a long pedigree. In its earlier manifestations the critique of American mass culture was highly explicit and had to be. Many ominous trends of an evolving mass culture in Europe had to be shown to have originated in America, reaching Europe under clear American agency. An intellectual repertoire of Americanism and Americanization evolved in a continuing attempt at cultural resistance against the lures of a culture of consumption. Never mind that such cultural forms might have come to Europe autonomously, even in the absence of an American model. America served to give a name and a face to forces of cultural change that would otherwise have been anonymous and seemingly beyond control.

Today this European repertoire is alive and kicking. Yet, ironically, the repertoire has become common currency to the point of being an intellectual stereotype rather than an informed opinion; America nowadays is often a subtext, unspoken in European forms of cultural resistance. A recent example may serve to illustrate this. A political poster for the Socialist Party in Salzburg, in the run-up to municipal elections in the city, shows us the determined face and the clenched fist of the party's candidate. He asks the voting public whether the younger generation will not be losers, and calls on the electorate to "fight, fight, and fight." What for? "In order to avoid that young people will get fed up with the future" (Damit unsere Jugend die Zukunft nicht satt hat). In a visual

Political campaign poster, Salzburg, 1997.

pun, at the poster's dead center, getting "fed up" is illustrated by the blurred image of a hamburger flying by at high speed. Fast food indeed. The call for action is now clear. Austrians should try to fend off a future cast in an American vein. American culture is condensed into the single image of the hamburger, the symbol of a culture centered on consumption rather than consummation. It is enough to trigger the larger repertoire of cultural anti-Americanism.

We may choose to see this poster as only a recent version of cultural guardianship that has always looked at the younger generation as a stalking horse, if not a Trojan horse, for American culture. In fact, historically, it has always been younger generations who, in rebellion against parental authority and cultural imposition, have opted for the liberating potential of American mass culture. Yet interesting changes may have occurred in this pattern. Today young people as well, in their concern about forces of globalization, may target America as the central agency behind these global trends. They may smash the windows of a nearby McDonald's (and there is always a McDonald's nearby), they may deface equestrian statues in Turin, or may choose more creative and subtle forms of protest. Yet again America tends to be a mere subtext in their resistance against global cultural icons.

One more example may serve to illustrate this. I have a music video, a few years old, of a Basque group. The video, in its own right, is an act of cultural emancipation. The lyrics are in the Basque language, and the station broadcasting the video had all-Basque programming. This may suggest localism, if not cultural provincialism. Nothing would be further from the truth. What we have here is a perfect example of "glocalisation," to use Roland Robertson's neologism.[13] The music used is ska, an ingredient of "world music" hailing from the Caribbean and popularized through the British music industry. The format of the music video itself is part of global musical entertainment. Yet the message is local. What the video shows is a confusing blend of the traditional and the modern. The opening shot is of a man using a scythe to cut grass. The camera moves up and shows a modern, international-style office block. A mobile phone rings, and the grass cutter answers the call. More images show modern life. We see an old man talking into a microphone strapped to his head, as if he is talking to himself. We see a group of young men on a flatbed lorry moving through traffic. They are working out in tandem on treadmill machines, yet in complete isolation, like a transported glimpse of an American gym. Then the protagonists of the video appear, with a rickety van, getting ready to sell the local variety of Basque fast food, a sausage on a roll. The very smell breaks the isolation of the people caught in the alienating life of modernity. They all flock to the sausage stand to get a taste of true Basqueness. They come to life in a celebration of a quasi-authentic form of traditional Basque life. The lyrics repeat the refrain: "Down with McDonald's, Long live Big Benat [the name of the Basque delicacy]."

The claim made in this video is on behalf of the authenticity of regional cultures struggling to survive in a world threatened by the homogenizing forces of globalization. Yet the medium of communication testifies to the impact of precisely those forces as much as it protests against them. In that sense the video is a perfect example of glocalization. There is much irony in all this, but most important is the fact that what is shown as modernity truly revives a long repertoire of European cultural anti-Americanism. America *is* modernity, and the long history of European resistance to America is truly a story of resisting the onslaught of modernity on Europe's checkered map of regional and/or national cultures.

To watch this ambiguous proclamation of a regional culture's superiority and authenticity is to be reminded again of the irony of life in today's many liminal Europes, literally at the *limes,* the edge, of Europe's cultural sway. As one visit to Bilbao, the industrial city in the Basque country, will make clear, the Basqueness of the place is, if anything, an imposed and unduly homogenized reading. Under the impact of industrialization Bilbao, like so many other industrial centers, has drawn its workforce from a large hinterland, forgetful of the integrity of local culture. If capitalism, as Joseph Schumpeter reminded us long ago, is a force of creative destruction, Bilbao testifies to the truth of this statement. People from all over Spain have migrated there and lived there for several generations, giving the place a multicultural tone, and eroding Basqueness from within its own territory. Following years of decline, the city has now revived. In addition to restoring its heritage of a residential and industrial architecture redolent of its past prowess, it has also sought to reconnect itself to the contemporary modernity of cutting-edge architecture. By the river that runs through the city now stands one of Europe's great modern structures, a museum of art designed by the American architect Frank Gehry and financed by Guggenheim money. With its wavy lines it evokes a local seafaring history and seems to mirror the river that connected Bilbao to the wider world. It is a modern rendition of a local history that lives on as collective memory. It seems to have sprouted from that store of memories, much as the creative genius who shaped it lives across the ocean's waters that wash the Basque coast at their eastern reach. If Bilbao seeks to reconnect itself to a cosmopolitanism it once reflected, its strivings stand at right angles to the efforts at freezing Basqueness in time. Whatever the peculiarities of this tension, its inherent logic makes Bilbao a microcosm of Europe's many internal contradictions.

EIGHT ◉ SHOCK AND AWE IN NEW YORK CITY

*9/11 or 9-1-1? The Construction of Terrorism
through Photographs*

I WAS ON THE PHONE when it happened. I was talking to my wife across the Atlantic from Boston. I had flown in the previous night from Washington, D.C., to Logan Airport. My landlady came up, frantically gesticulating. "Rob, come, you must see this." I followed her to the TV room and stood transfixed. One of the towers of the World Trade Center in New York was ablaze. Then a plane, ever so tiny it seemed, slammed into the second tower, exploding in a burst of fire and debris. It was an arresting moment, and my mind duly froze it. My thoughts, like those of everyone watching this, instantly went out to what must be going on inside the towers, to people trapped on floors above the level of impact, to others trying to escape the inferno. There were a few images of people jumping to their self-chosen deaths, tiny figurines tumbling down—yet, as I remember them, forever suspended in flight. As I watched the fires rage, there were eerie moments of déjà vu, of Hollywood images popping up, almost instantly, yet inadmissibly, aestheticizing the spectacle. I stood ashamed at my own train of associations. Then, as I remember it in almost slow motion, the giant towers imploded, one after the other. There were images of people in the streets, running for cover, chased by a billowing cloud of dust and smoke.

The rest of that day images of the disaster were replayed over and over again on all major channels. Yet some instant editing took place. Images of people falling, unavoidable in the initial direct reporting, were, if shown at all, carefully contextualized, as in the case of two people holding hands as they tumbled down. In one therapeutic talk show, the falling couple was seen as an emblem of human grandeur far transcending the inhumanity of the terrorists. Yet the bulk of the images being replayed were those of the second plane coming up and hitting the second tower, strangely naturalizing the event as if it were a matter of a volcano bursting, causing death and devastation. Images of people running, the awareness of people missing, of thousands dead, of others bereft and grieving, stories of heroic rescue actions by firemen, produced an instant narrative of cataclysm, an emergency of stupendous proportions. It caused an outpouring of solidarity, of people thronging to give blood, of wakes all over town to help people cope with grief and revive the bonds of community. Old memories of heroism in the face of disaster inspired public rituals, as in the case of firemen raising a flag on the rubble of the Twin Towers while taking their choreographic cues from the famous Iwo Jima photograph by AP staff photographer Joe Rosenthal.[1]

Television images may have produced the "flashbulb memory" of the event that millions share, yet photography played an indispensable role in anchoring the moment in individual memory. It did so in a number of ways. Photojournalists rushed out to document the disaster. Some could not reach the site and took panoramic photographs from across the Hudson or East River, freezing consecutive dramatic moments in the midst of a Manhattan skyline that looked otherwise unperturbed. Others managed to get close and were able to put a human face to the disaster. The evening newspapers of that day to a larger extent than they normally do relied on photographic witness. Within days many newspapers brought out special editions, prominently featuring photographs documenting the attack on the towers as well as the public's response to it. Part of the response in days following September 11 crucially centered on photography. People wandered about Ground Zero holding up photographs of dear ones that were missing, and before long the *New York Times* would publish a daily section with photographs of individuals killed in the towers' collapse, accompanied by short biographical notes.

Also, by late November, a variety of 9/11-related exhibitions had been quickly organized, especially in New York, where local audiences were in need of collective, therapeutic relief from the trauma they had suffered. The displays were constantly crowded. Some, like a museum show that featured the work of members of the elite Magnum Photos news agency (who happened to be in town for their annual meeting on the weekend preceding 9/11), were exclusive; others, like "This Is New York: A Democracy of Photographs," were radically inclusive and unedited. Any snapshot taken that day was accepted.

In the nature of such responses to urgent emotional needs, many of these displays were transient. Shows came to an end; newspapers were discarded. Yet a range of publications preserved selected images for later use. As selections, though, they pose their own problems for the collective memory of the event and its impact. On this point, in a collection published by Magnum Photos, Thomas Hoepker, vice president of Magnum, has this to say:

> I strongly believe in documentary photography, in taking pictures of real life.
> When I looked at the pictures from our photographers, there were some that were wonderful or clever compositions, but they emphasized the artistry in photography rather than telling the story. We didn't put those pictures in this book. I don't think they belong in this book because they do not serve its purpose, which is to bear witness. In a moment like this you must be very humble. When something like this happens, nothing you do can adequately respond to the monstrosity of the event.[2]

He himself had been unable to make it to Manhattan and was stuck on the other side of the East River. From there he took photographs, several of which are reproduced in the Magnum volume, of a stark Dantesque quality, showing downtown Manhattan engulfed in an unspeakable inferno. One, tellingly, has a cemetery in the foreground, sunlit and peaceful, with a shrouded Manhattan farther off. Yet in the case of his own photographs Hoepker apparently used criteria for selection other than the one of unwanted artistry. One of his photographs from across the river shows a group of young people taking a rest, chatting, having a drink, a bicycle parked in their midst. They are relaxed and have their backs turned toward the Manhattan inferno, displaying utter disinterest in what is happening. This too, of course, was part of the public response, yet not a part that Hoepker wished to integrate into his construction of the memorable. The photograph, I assume with Hoepker's permission, was included in a volume titled *Underexposed.* As the editor, Colin Jacobson, explains the point of the book, it "investigates some of the most glaring examples of photographs which have been banned, doctored, suppressed or manipulated in order to dupe the viewer."[3] The volume had initially been planned as a special issue of *Index on Censorship,* an international magazine that had for thirty years devoted itself to defending free expression. In the volume as it was then separately produced, Hoepker's image is the concluding example in a collection of hundreds of photographs meant to reveal the hidden history of the twentieth century through "photographs the public weren't supposed to see."[4]

We will never know the full extent of the self-censorship and manipulation behind the public construction of disaster striking downtown Manhattan, of the many ways of bearing witness and of responding to what, from one perspective, was an emergency. From that perspective 9/11 may well read as 911. The emergency telephone number must have rung deafeningly on that momentous day. One way to restore a more comprehensive historical record is to assemble as many of the public's responses as possible and to save them from transience. True to its mission to serve as the nation's memory bank, the Library of Congress initiated a massive effort to collect the full range of public responses to and reflections of the emergency, ranging from pictorial images, newspapers, special newspaper editions, and digital materials put out on the Web to taped interviews conducted by professional ethnographers, teachers, and students with accompanying written documentation and photographs of memorials to the victims of the attacks from around the United States.[5] Newspapers came in from all over the world. Special editions or sections published on September 11 and 12 bear banner headlines screaming "Terror," "Horror," "Infamy," "Bastards," "Apocalypse." They veer between the extremes of initial response, the sense of shock at an apocalyptic emergency on the one hand, and the first outraged recognition of agency, of willful attack, on the other. Old memories of vulnerability came up, as in the *Honolulu Advertiser's* September 12 headline: "America's bloodiest day, 'This is the second Pearl Harbor.'"

The Library of Congress staff cast its net even wider in order to include the totally different response of exhilaration at what had happened in expressions of an entrenched anti-Americanism in certain parts of the Islamic world. The most remarkable of such documents, a Pakistani poster obtained in October 2001, depicts Bin Laden against the backdrop of the World Trade Center under attack. The poster is significant because it appears to represent an early claim of responsibility for the assault on the towers by Bin Laden or his followers and sympathizers in Pakistan. The primary caption, in Urdu, translates: "Hundreds of Osamas will emerge from every drop of my blood." Even today it reads like a chilling prophecy.

Soon, as we all remember, the reading of the September 11 events in terms of agency, of "evildoers," of terrorists, would come to prevail, giving direction and purpose to America's response to the terrorist attack. America engaged in a war on terrorism, geographically situating a threat that was inherently transnational and hydra-headed. For some photojournalists the transition was smooth. They went from shooting the events on September 11 to covering American military engagement in Afghanistan, as in the case of *New York Times* staff photographers Vincent Laforet, James Hill, Tyler Hicks, and Ruth Fremson. *New York Times* photographer Kelly Guenther and her colleague Steve Ludlum, a freelancer working for the *Times,* had taken Pulitzer Prize–winning photographs of the second plane approaching the second tower, and then of its devastating impact. Ludlum's picture froze that moment in time, the inferno, the rainfall of shattered debris, the first smoking tower in the background. Their Pulitzer award was for Spot Breaking News. The team that went on to Pakistan and Afghanistan won the Pulitzer Feature News Photography award. It was the first time in Pulitzer history that one publication captured both photo Pulitzers.[6]

To me at least, there is something oddly jarring between performing the job of bearing witness on behalf of the general public, done in a spirit, as Thomas Hoepker reminds us, of self-effacing humility, and the lionization of individual photographers through Pulitzer Prizes or similar awards. It is suggestive of a blurring of individual motives in the minds of photojournalists. While joining a collective endeavor of bearing witness, with all the feelings of humility this entails, are they at the same time engaged in a highly individual contest, consciously vying for primacy of place? If so, the latter motive seems to take away from the spirit of public mission. This may sound like old-fashioned sniping, echoing a nostalgia for the times of selfless, if not anonymous, effort in the public interest, the style of journalism without authorial attribution that still characterizes newspapers like the London *Economist*. Yet in our age of competitive professionalism the quest for individual excellence and public recognition, instituted in our prize rituals, does undeniably play a role in determining the way that photographs enter the public realm and affect our collective memory. Prizewinning photographs more likely gain iconic status. Their mass circulation is given a boost; many more people become aware of them and integrate them in their recollections of historic events.

Tellingly, in the case of the Pulitzer Prizes, the Spot Breaking News and the Feature News categories were connected. Photographers followed a trail set out by the American government's response to the breaking news at the World Trade Center. They saw it as their mission to give the American public a visual sense of what the world looked like in places that provided the terrorists with their safe haven. Rather than trying to project a view of terrorism as crucially transnational, of interconnected cells that had metastasized internationally, they adopted the nation-state reading that the American government had chosen as the focus for its response. Thus, in Afghanistan, to quote Hall Buell's words: "[T]hey photographed an ancient world locked in a medieval lifestyle by a repressive regime of religious fanatics."[7] It is a choice of words that informed much of the public representation, in America and more generally the West, of Afghanistan at the time. Intervening there, America saw it as its dual assignment not only to punish the terrorists but also to bring freedom and democracy to a country "locked in a medieval lifestyle" against its will. A sense of dual assignment for America inspired action in Afghanistan first, in Iraq (with much less international support) later. A foreign-policy doctrine formulating this dual mission as America's unilateral agenda, to act preemptively in self-defense while bringing democracy in the wake of intervention, would be officially codified in a post-Afghanistan White House document on the new national security strategy, published in September 2002.[8]

President Bush and his foreign-policy team may have fully come into their own after September 11. The event gave them collectively their "flashbulb" view of the central challenge to America's place in the world. I vividly remember watching the flashbulb go off in President Bush's mind when he was told of the WTC attack while visiting a school in Florida. On television, or later in Michael Moore's *Fahrenheit 911*, you could see the news sink in. He surely will remember where he was when he first heard the news. His initial reaction betrayed an unsure touch. It took a while for him to find a response and a role. It reminded me of my own initial response to the news of President Kennedy's assassination. I had arrived for an evening's gathering of my student fraternity in Amsterdam and was told the news. Being handed a bottle of beer, I remember my first response as one of utter inadequacy. I had a sense of "Oh well, let's move on to what we came here for." It was not until the next day, when I had gone home to spend the weekend with my parents, that I saw the assassination on television. Only then did the portent of what had happened dawn on me and I sat sobbing in front of the TV set, ashamed at the inadequacy of my initial response, while being overwhelmed by the flood of images from Dallas and the manifold responses of Americans to the loss of their president, so much more adequate than mine. All this makes up my flashbulb memory of the Kennedy assassination, some of it highly private and individual, some of it shared with others. Some of it a matter of inner mental pictures, putting myself into the remembered episode, some of it highly mediated through television and newspaper photographs, of Jacqueline Kennedy bending over her mortally wounded husband in the open limousine, or of her standing in utter desolation next to Lyndon Johnson as he was sworn in as Kennedy's successor. Which of these mediated images do I remember best? Probably the still photographs, although I cannot get the crucial moments from the Zapruder film, replayed so often over the years, from my mind. Definitely, a short film clip, moments of motion, are part of my flashbulb memory.

As I remember it, my reading of the Dallas assassination was one of tragedy, of emergency. I was never much bothered by the question of who had done it. When Lee Harvey Oswald was caught, then killed, that to me was the end of it. The rest was research work, in the Kennedy case for the Warren Commission, in the World Trade Center case for international police and intelligence agents to roll up cells of al-Qaeda, quietly, unspectacularly. Conspiracy theorists love to see hydra-headed monsters, only to go out and chop off their heads. In the Kennedy case such theories may never have held water in the first place. In the case of Al-Qaeda they crucially do, which to me seems all the more reason not to go about chopping off heads, but getting the beast by the tail.

I happened to be in New York the day that the events of the year before were being remembered in a moving, simple ceremony. Again it
came to me via television. The list of names was being read of all those
who had lost their lives in the towering inferno of the World Trade Center. Their names appropriately reflect what the words *World Trade Center* conjure up; they are names of people from all over the world, from
Africa, the Middle East, the Far East, the Pacific, Latin America, Europe, and of course North America—people of many cultures and many
religions. Again the whole world was watching, and I suddenly realized
that something remarkable was happening. On that day, the American
mass media recorded an event staged by Americans. Americans powerfully reappropriated a place where a year ago international terrorism had
been in charge. They literally turned the site into a *lieu de mémoire.* They
were, in the words of Lincoln's Gettysburg Address, read again on this
occasion, consecrating the place. They imbued it with the sense and
meaning of a typically American scripture. It is the language that, for
more than two centuries, has defined America's purpose and mission in
the ringing words of freedom and democracy.

I borrow the words "American scripture" from Michael Ignatieff. He
used them in a piece he wrote for a special issue of *Granta.*[9] He is one
of twenty-four writers from various parts of the world who contributed
to a section titled "What We Think of America." Ignatieff describes
American scripture as "the treasure house of language, at once sacred
and profane, to renew the faith of the only country on earth . . . whose
citizenship is an act of faith, the only country whose promises to itself
continue to command the faith of people like me, who are not its citizens." Ignatieff is a Canadian. He describes a faith and an affinity with
American hopes and dreams that many non-Americans share. Yet, if it
was the point of *Granta*'s editors to explore the question of "Why others hate us, Americans," Ignatieff's view is not of much help. In the outside world after 9/11, as *Granta*'s editor, Ian Jack, reminds us, there was
a widespread feeling that "Americans had it coming to them," that it was
"good that Americans now know what it's like to be vulnerable." For
people who share such views American scripture deconstructs into
hypocrisy and willful deceit.

There are many signs in the recent past of people's views of America
shifting in the direction of disenchantment and disillusionment. Sure
enough, there were fine moments when President Bush rose to the oc-

casion and used the hallowed words of American scripture to make it clear to the world and his fellow Americans what terrorism had truly attacked. The terrorists' target had been more than symbols of American power and prowess. It had been the very values of freedom and democracy that America sees as its foundation. These were moments when the president literally seemed to rise above himself. But it was never long before he showed a face of America that had already worried many longtime friends and allies during Bush's first year in office, to say nothing of the way he was, not elected, but selected.

Even before September 11, the Bush administration had signaled its retreat from the internationalism that had consistently inspired U.S. foreign policy since World War II, if not before.[10] Ever since Woodrow Wilson, American scripture had also come to imply the vision of a world order that would forever transcend the lawlessness of international relations. Many of the international organizations that now serve to regulate interstate relations bear a markedly American imprint, and spring from American ideals and initiatives. President Bush Sr., in spite of his avowed aversion to the "vision thing," nevertheless deemed it essential to speak of a New World Order when at the end of the Cold War Saddam Hussein's invasion of Kuwait seemed to signal a relapse into a state of international lawlessness. Bush Jr. took a narrower, national-interest view of America's place in the world. In an unabashed unilateralism he moved U.S. foreign policy away from high-minded idealism and the arena of international treaty obligations. He actively undermined the fledgling International Criminal Court in The Hague, rather than taking a leadership role in making it work. He displayed a consistent unwillingness to play by rules internationally agreed and to abide by decisions reached by international bodies that the United States itself had helped set up. He squarely placed the United States above or outside the reach of international law, seeing himself as the sole and final arbiter of America's national interest.

After September 11 this outlook only hardened. The Bush administration's overriding view of international relations in terms of the war against terrorism has led the United States to ride roughshod over its own constitutional protection of civil rights as well as over international treaty obligations under the Geneva Convention in the ways it handles individuals, U.S. citizens among them, suspected of links to terrorist networks. Seeing antiterrorism as the one way to define who is with America or against it, President Bush takes forms of state terrorism, whether in Russia against the Chechens or in Israel against the Palestinians, as so many justified antiterrorist efforts. He gives them his full support and called Sharon a "man of peace." If Europeans beg to differ and wish to take a more balanced view of the Israeli-Palestinian conflict, the Bush administration and many op-ed voices blame European anti-Semitism.

How have Europeans and Americans come to drift so far apart in their views of the centrality of the Palestinian/Israeli conflict and of how to handle it? Do we watch different television programs? Do we see different photographs in the press? Or do we read them differently? On several occasions during the Balkan wars of the 1990s it was the public outcry following the dissemination via television and the press of images of atrocities taking place there that led to joint American-European intervention with widespread public support, in Bosnia first, in Kosovo later. The atrocity photographs instantly triggered collective memories of the vast store of Holocaust pictures, which, after the fact, had educated Europeans and Americans on the enormity of the Nazi extermination policies. Such memories made for a reading of what was going on in the Balkans and a collective sense of "Not again." A modicum of peace has been restored in the Balkans, and we saw photographs of a tight-lipped Milosevic, the former Serbian president, facing an international tribunal in The Hague. It all seems a perfect replay of the horrors of World War II and of the Nuremberg trial. But the Balkans may be the wrong template for the war on terrorism.

No longer do photographs of terrorist acts by Palestinians in Israel or of Israeli retaliation make for a joint reading in Europe and the United States of what is going on, or for a joint sense of how jointly to intervene. This may have critically to do with different stores of World War II memories and images in Europe and the United States. One such store that informs the current European reading of images from the Middle East is one shared by continental Europeans but absent in Britain and the United States. It is formed by memories of occupation, resistance, collaboration, of German roundups of the Jewish population first, of able-bodied men later to be sent as forced labor to factories in Germany, of indiscriminate German retaliation following targeted assassinations of high-ranking Germans by the resistance in France, the Netherlands, Czechoslovakia.

I have one flashbulb memory of a German roundup—a *razzia,* as it was commonly known at the time—in the street in Haarlem where I lived. A German soldier entered our house, telling my mother that according to the neighbors, known collaborators, there must be a young man in the house. He must have been referring to my father, who was hiding under the floorboards. I was standing on a chair by the table, clinging to my mother, my heart pounding in my throat. My mother, in her best German, explained that her husband was out of town, trying to find food for the family. The German turned to me and said: "Shall I take you then?" It must have been a cruel joke, or at least that is the twist my mother gave it, in an effort to reassure and protect me. Yet a flashbulb went off in my mind, forever burning the moment into my brain.

Yet is has taken long for memories of occupation to begin to affect the European reading of the Palestinian-Israeli conflict, for obvious reasons. For one thing, there was the other store of Holocaust images, mixed in with collective guilt and shame over the fate of Europe's Jews. This made for a ready, if not facile, sense of Israel's legitimacy, and for support during the decades when it was a fragile entity threatened by a surrounding Arab world. Sympathy for the underdog played a role as well. Then, in the late 1960s, slowly a shift in perception began to occur. Peace treaties with Egypt and Jordan eroded the sense of Arab homogeneity. A sense of there being a Palestinian nation with its legitimate rights slowly formed, in Europe as well as in United Nations discourse. Slowly a sense took hold of Palestinians living under Israeli occupation, ever since the 1967 Six Day War, and of Israeli governments and citizens doing things in occupied territories, through annexation and settlement, that flew in the face of international law. People in Europe who had resisted South Africa's treatment of its black population became aware of vexing parallels with Israeli policies. It became increasingly hard to see Israel, the foremost military power in the Middle East, as the underdog. Increasingly Palestinians came to be seen as a victimized population. Images of World War II occupation and of Jewish persecution began to merge and to apply to the ordeal of the Palestinians. Nothing of the sort has happened in the United States, at least not on the level of informed journalism, public opinion, or government policies. It is history as remembered, as offering lessons for the reading of the present, that has driven a tragic wedge between American and European views of what is the case in the Middle East. Trying to square the vicious circle of terrorism and counterterrorism in the Middle East, the United States may well end up being sucked into the vicious circle. Before too long we may all witness, through television images and photographs, a sequel to September 11, 2001.

In its war on terrorism the United States has chosen to widen its aim and, applying its doctrine of preemptive war, to invade Iraq. Its case for intervention relentlessly eroded as no weapons of mass destruction were found, and none of the alleged links between Saddam Hussein and al-Qaeda could be established. One moral justification for the war, though, still stands: to rid the Iraqi people of a heinous regime and to bring democracy to the country. Even that moral high ground eroded beyond repair when digital images from the Abu Ghraib prison got out for all to see. More than any previous reports—including those of the International Red Cross about the way the United States infringed on international law in its treatment of enemy combatants, keeping them in legal limbo—these visual images shattered the moral authority of the United States. They may turn out to be the latter-day equivalent of Nick Ut's photograph of the napalmed girl in Vietnam.

When I saw these digital images I was reminded of the use of photographs in America's cultural diplomacy in the years of the Cold War. In the traveling exhibition "The Family of Man," and in the short-lived attempt at the Brussels World's Fair to show the world that in terms of civil rights there was still unfinished business left for the United States to work on, photographic evidence deployed by the U.S. State Department was meant to counter the impact of pictures of race discrimination in the American South. Newspapers across the globe had shown images from Mississippi and Little Rock that had caused many people to reconsider the moral basis of the United States' claim to leadership of the Free World. The difference with the pictures taken of the Abu Ghraib abominations and disseminated worldwide is clear. What people in the United States, in Europe, in the Middle East now behold are images of an unspeakable moral lapse taking place *under the direct authority* of the United States government, a lapse that the highest authorities are unwilling fully to own up to. The United States, militarily deployed in Afghanistan and Iraq, urgently needs the soft power of cultural diplomacy to project the values that have so often inspired America's foreign policy. But it now finds itself with empty hands. If anything, it has managed to place itself outside the family of man.

Notes

Introduction (pp. 1–6)

1. Roland Barthes, *La Chambre Claire: Note sur la photographie* (Paris: Gallimard, Le Seuil, 1980), pp. 99–128.
2. Raymond Queneau, *Exercices de style* (Paris: Gallimard, 1947).
3. Alan Trachtenberg, *Reading American Photographs: Images as History, Mathew Brady to Walker Evans* (New York: Farrar, Strauss, and Giroux, 1990).
4. Robert Frank, *The Americans* (New York: Grove Press, 1959). Originally published as *Les américains* (Paris: Robert Delpire, 1958).
5. Jean Back and Viktoria Schmidt-Linsenhoff, eds., *The Family of Man, 1955–2001. Humanism and Postmodernism: A Reappraisal of the Photo Exhibition by Edward Steichen* (Marburg: Jonas Verlag, 2004).
6. Michael Shulan, "Introduction," in *Here Is New York: A Democracy of Photographs* (Zurich/Berlin/New York, 2002), p. 8.

Chapter 1. Arresting Moments (pp. 7–33)

1. L. R. Brown and J. Kulik, "Flashbulb Memories," *Cognition* 5 (1977): 73–99. Also M. Conway, *Flashbulb Memories* (Hilsdale, N.J.: L. Erlbaum Associates, 1995).
2. Rebecca Solnit, *Motion Studies: Time, Place and Eadweard Muybridge* (London: Bloomsbury, 2003).
3. Of course, Marker's film can only be construed as an extreme here, of film returning to its origin in still photographs, given the logic of my argument. In terms of dramatic impact, there is a world of difference between motion freezing into one still picture and films consisting of one long series of still photographs. Related to this, Ansel Adams tells an amusing anecdote. One day, in 1944, he was invited by David O. Selznick, of Selznick Productions in Hollywood, to try out a "revolutionary new idea," i.e., to make fine prints of individual black-and-white frames from film reels, to be used as publicity photographs. It all came to naught. As Adams has it: "Finis to my role in the revolutionary

concept of still photographs taken from the original negative film." Ansel Adams, *An Autobiography* (Boston/New York/London: Little, Brown, and Company, 1996), pp. 94–95.

4. In a remarkable exhibition photo historian Geoffrey Batchen explores this photographic practice, bringing together hundreds of photographs used as mementos. Often markers are added, such as wreaths enveloping the picture, to emphasize its new meaning as a memento for the deceased. Often such memorial arrangements are photographed again, in a photographic practice that is truly Batchen's central interest. Geoffrey Batchen, *Forget Me Not: Photography and Remembrance* (New York: Princeton Architectural Press, 2004).

5. Gregor Krause and Karl With, *Bali: Volk und Kunst,* 2 vols. (Hagen: Folkwang Verlag, 1920. Reprinted in a one-volume, condensed edition in 1922. Reissued in English, with an introduction by Hugh H. Mabbett, as *Bali 1912* (Wellington, New Zealand: January Books, 1988). A revised edition was published in 2001 by Pepper Publications, Singapore. Also Gregor Krause, *Borneo* 3 vols. (München: G. Müller, 1926).

Chapter 2. Photography and Immigration (pp. 34–56)

1. W. G. Sebald, *The Emigrants,* translated from German by Michael Hulse (New York: New Directions Publishing Corporation, 1997).

2. Stieglitz's "The Steerage" has acquired its iconic status as a picture of immigrants in spite of the fact that most likely the steerage passengers that he photographed were return migrants. Stieglitz was on his way to Europe when he took the photograph.

3. Louis Adamic, *Laughing in the Jungle* (New York: Harper and Row, 1932), as quoted in Th. L. Gross, ed., *A Nation of Nations: Ethnic Literature in America* (New York: The Free Press, 1971), p. 81.

4. P. Cresci, *Il pane dalle sette croste* (Lucca, 1986), p. 239.

5. James C. Schaap, "The Heritage of These Many Years," in *Sign of Promise and Other Stories* (Sioux Center, Iowa: Dordt College Press, 1979), pp. 248ff.

6. Willem Wilterdink, *Winterswijkse pioniers in Amerika* (Winterswijk: Vereniging 'Het Museum,' 1990), pp. 32ff.

7. The largest collection of letters to be published is W. Helbich, W. D. Kamphoefner, and U. Sommer, eds., *Briefe aus Amerika: Deutsche Auswanderer schreiben aus der neuen Welt, 1830–1930* (München: Verlag C. H. Beck, 1988).

8. See, e.g., my book *The Persistence of Ethnicity: Dutch Calvinist Pioneers in Amsterdam, Montana* (Urbana/Champaign and Chicago: University of Illinois Press, 1992).

9. Herbert J. Brinks, *Schrijf spoedig terug: Brieven van immigranten in Amerika, 1847–1920* (The Hague: Uitgeverij Boekencentrum, 1978); also avail-

able in an English translation: *Write Back Soon: Letters from Immigrants in America* (Grand Rapids, Michigan: CRC Publications, 1986).

10. The writer uses the Dutch word *lijkenis,* which is an unusual synonym for portrait.

11. I have used single quotation marks for those passages that were in English. Even the use of Dutch, though, shows the impact of English after so many years as an immigrant in the United States. The letter was written by one of two sisters (with the family name "Tacoma") to her nephew in Friesland in the Netherlands. This sister had migrated from Friesland and had not seen the other sister, who had stayed behind, for many years. By the time she received the photos mentioned in her letter, she had moved from Yakima to Santa Monica, California.

12. From: H. Ganzevoort and M. Boekelman, *Dutch Immigration to North-America* (Toronto: The Multi-Cultural Historical Society of Ontario, 1983).

13. Schaap, *Sign of Promise,* pp. 61–81.

Chapter 3. The History of Photography and the Photography of History
(pp. 57–82)

1. Peter C. Marzio, *The Democratic Art: Pictures for a 19th-Century America* (Boston: David R. Godine Publisher, 1979), p. xi.

2. James Bryce, *Studies in Contemporary Biography* (New York: Macmillan Co., 1903), p. 372.

3. Daniel J. Boorstin, *The Image, or What Happened to the American Dream* [1962] (Middlesex: Penguin Books, 1963), chapter 1.

4. See his classic treatment of what happens to art in the era of mass reproduction: "Das Kunstwerk im Zeitalter seiner technischen Reproduzierbarkeit," in Walter Benjamin, *Illuminationen: Ausgewählte Schriften* (Frankfurt am Main: Suhrkamp Verlag, 1977), pp. 136–170.

5. For an exploration of this man-made version of the sublime, see David Nye, *American Technological Sublime* (Cambridge, Massachusetts: MIT Press, 1994).

6. On this particular aspect of the use that immigrants made of photography, see the previous chapter.

7. *Berliner Illustrierte Zeitung* 21, 1930; p. 949.

8. *Berliner Illustrierte Zeitung* 22, 1930; p. 958.

9. On this aspect of the rationalization of distribution and consumption under American auspices, following earlier stages of the rationalization of production, see George Ritzer, *The McDonaldization of Society* (Boston: Pine Forge Press, 1993).

10. Quoted by David E. Haberstich, "American Photographs in Europe and

Illusions of Travel," in D. E. Nye and M. Gidley, eds., *American Photographs in Europe* (Amsterdam: VU University Press, 1994), p. 59.

11. Quoted by Maren Kröger, "From Sublime Vision to 'The Thing in Itself': American Art Photography at German Exhibitions, 1893–1929," in Nye and Gidley, *American Photographs in Europe*, p. 96.

12. Ansel Adams, *An Autobiography* (Boston/New York/London: Little, Brown and Company, 1996), p. 90. Also Mary Street Alinder, *Ansel Adams: A Biography* (New York: Henry Holt and Company, 1996), pp. 87, 88. According to Alinder, all or most of the one-page manifesto was written by Adams.

13. On this, see Jean Kempf, "American Photography in France since World War II: Was France Liberated by the United States?" in Nye and Gidley, *American Photographs in Europe*, pp. 210, 218.

14. Alain Mons, *La traversée du visible: Images et lieux du contemporain* (Paris: Les Editions de la Passion, 2002), p. 32.

15. Ibid., p. 30.

16. Alan Trachtenberg, *Reading American Photographs: Images as History, Mathew Brady to Walker Evans* (New York: Farrar, Strauss, and Giroux, 1990).

17. For a selection of these photographs and background information, see Colin Jacobson, *Underexposed* (New York: Vision On Publishing, 2002), pp. 172–173.

18. Ibid., pp. 156–157.

19. *World without End: Photography and the 20th Century* (Sydney: Art Gallery of New South Wales, 2000), p. 111.

20. Quoted in Edward Wakin, *Photos That Made US History, Vol. II: From the Cold War to the Space Age* (New York: Walker and Company, 1993), p. 23.

21. There have been those who argued that the Tet Offensive may have been a public opinion coup for North Vietnam, while militarily it was a disaster for the North. See, e.g., Peter Braestrup, *Big Story: How the U.S. Press and Television Reported and Analyzed the Tet Crisis of 1968* (Boulder, Colorado: Westview Press, 1977; New Haven/London: Yale University Press, 1983).

22. Vicky Goldberg and Robert Silberman, *American Photography: A Century of Images* (San Francisco: Chronicle Books, 1999), p. 219. The original photograph of the shooting is by Bob Jackson, 1963.

23. *World without End*, p. 110.

24. The firefighter is shown in the documentary film *9/11*, produced by Jules and Gedeon Naudet, two French documentary filmmakers who happened to be in New York making a film about one rookie firefighter who underwent his fire baptism on the day of 9/11. The film contains gripping footage from inside one of the burning towers. *9/11, The Filmmakers' Commemorative*, produced by Goldfish Pictures/Reveille/Silverstar Productions, 2001. DVD release by Paramount Pictures Corporation (Hollywood, 2002).

25. Ric Burns, *New York: The Center of the World, a Documentary Film* (Boston: WGBH, 2003), Episode Eight: 1946–2003.

26. Tom Junod, "The Falling Man," *Esquire* 140, 3 (September 2003).

27. http://www.newsday.com/news/nationaworld/wire/la-oe-drew10 sep10,0,2008868.story?coll=sns-ap-nationworld-headlines.

28. Junod, "The Falling Man."

29. Devin Zuber, "American Studies at Ground Zero: Walter Benjamin, Public Memory, and Memorial Aesthetics," paper presented at the John F. Kennedy Center for North-American Studies of the Free University in Berlin, February 12, 2005.

30. Art Spiegelman, *In the Shadow of No Towers* (New York: Pantheon Books, 2004).

31. For a subtle reading of Spiegelman's *In the Shadow of No Towers*, see Kries Versluys, "Art Spiegelman's *In the Shadow of No Towers:* 9/11 and the Experience of Trauma," paper presented at the Netherlands Institute for Advanced Studies (NIAS), March 2005.

Chapter 4. Faces of War (pp. 83–98)

1. Bill Brown, *The Material Unconscious: American Amusement, Stephen Crane, and the Economics of Play* (Cambridge, Massachusetts: Harvard University Press, 1996), p. 144.

2. "Photographic Phases," *New York Times*, July 21, 1862, p. 5.

3. Alan Trachtenberg, *Reading American Photographs: Images as History* (New York: Hill and Wang, 1989).

4. John C. Ropes, "The War as We See It Now," *Scribner's* 9 (June 1891): 778, 785.

5. Brown, *Material Unconscious*, p. 148.

6. See the discussion in chapter 2, footnote on pp. 38–39, regarding the way in which photography forever changed our way of seeing, compared with earlier forms of representational art.

7. See Amy Kaplan, "The Spectacle of War in Crane's Revision of History," in Lee Clark Mitchell, ed., *New Essays on the 'Red Badge of Courage'* (Cambridge: Cambridge University Press, 1986), pp.77–108. Taking Crane's writing as her case in point, she sees it as a revision of the popular view of war. A revision, though—as I shall be arguing—that could have been done only in the age of photography.

8. Oliver Wendell Holmes, "Doings of the Sunbeam," *Atlantic Monthly* 12 (July 1863): 11–12.

9. Oliver Wendell Holmes, "My Hunt after 'The Captain,'" *Atlantic Monthly*, December 1862, 738–764.

10. Christopher Benfey, *The Double Life of Stephen Crane* (New York: A. A. Knopf, 1992), p. 107.

11. As quoted in Carol Shloss, *In Visible Light: Photography and the American Writer, 1840–1940* (New York/Oxford: Oxford University Press, 1987), p. 17.

12. The quotation is almost a staple in the critical literature on Crane; see, for example, Milne Holton, *Cylinder of Vision: The Fiction and Journalistic Writings of Stephen Crane* (Baton Rouge: Louisiana State University Press, 1972), p. 10, or Sergio Perosa, "Naturalism and Impressionism in Stephen Crane's Fiction," in Maurice Bassan, ed., *Stephen Crane: A Collection of Critical Essays* (Englewood Cliffs, New Jersey: Prentice Hall, 1967), p. 92. About Crane's kind of impressionism Conrad had his doubts. In a letter to Edward Garnett, Conrad characterized Crane as "the *only* impressionist and *only* an impressionist." While this is a disparaging statement, expressive of Conrad's feeling of disappointment whenever he finished a book by Crane, Conrad in the same letter admired Crane's "amazing faculty of vision" (quoted by Michael Fried in *Realism, Writing, Disfiguration: On Thomas Eakins and Stephen Crane* (Chicago/London: University of Chicago Press, 1987), p. 183.

13. Fried, *Realism, Writing, Disfiguration,* p. 147.

14. Shloss, *In Visible Light,* p. 17.

15. See Benfey, *Double Life of Stephen Crane,* pp. 59–63.

16. According to Alan Trachtenberg in his *Reading American Photographs,* p. 78.

17. Ibid., p. 61.

18. Susan Sontag, "Writing Itself: On Roland Barthes," in Sontag, ed., *A Barthes Reader* (New York: Hill and Wang, 1982) p. xix.

19. Daniel Aaron, *The Unwritten War: American Writers and the Civil War* (New York: Oxford University Press, 1973) p. 215.

20. Benfey, *Double Life of Stephen Crane,* pp. 108, 109.

21. Ibid., p. 114.

22. William Frassanito, *Gettysburg: A Journey in Time* (New York: Scribner, 1975).

Chapter 5. Cold War Photography (pp. 99–128)

1. Roland Barthes, *La Chambre Claire: Note sur la photographie* (Paris: Gallimard, Le Seuil, 1980), pp. 47–51, 69–99.

2. L. Cohen, *A Consumers' Republic: The Politics of Mass Consumption in Postwar America* (New York: Alfred A. Knopf, 2003).

3. See John K. White, *Still Seeing Red: How the Cold War Shapes the New American Politics* (Boulder, Colorado: Westview Press, 1997). He based his research on the pool of public opinion data, the world's largest archive of survey data, gathered by the Roper Center for Public Opinion Research, at the campus of the University of Connecticut in Storrs.

4. Louis Hartz, *The Liberal Tradition in America* (New York: Harcourt, Brace, Jovanovich, 1955).

5. Arthur M. Schlesinger, Jr., *The Vital Center* (Boston: Houghton Mifflin Company, 1949), p. 244.

6. Frances S. Saunders, *The Cultural Cold War: The CIA and the World of Arts and Letters* (New York: New Press, 2000).

7. The joke is not mine, but Reinhold Wagnleitner's. See his "The Irony of American Culture Abroad," in Lary May, ed., *Recasting America* (Chicago: University of Chicago Press, 1989). pp. 285–301.

8. On this topic, see David Ellwood and Rob Kroes, eds., *Hollywood in Europe: Experiences of a Cultural Hegemony* (Amsterdam: VU University Press, 1994).

9. Saunders, *Cultural Cold War*, p. 193.

10. On this, see ibid., chapter 16. Also Erika Doss, *Benton, Pollock, and the Politics of Modernism: From Regionalism to Abstract Expressionism* (Chicago/London: University of Chicago Press, 1991).

11. http://www.uic.edu/~pbhales/Gottscho.html.

12. Peter B. Hales, "Picturing Levittown: Gottscho-Schleisner's Architectural and Commercial Photographs of Levittown, Long Island, 1947–1958," tigger.uic.edu~pbhales/Gottscho.html.

13. Alan Brinkley, "The Illusion of Unity in Cold War Culture," in Peter J. Kuznick and James Gilbert, eds., *Rethinking Cold War Culture* (Washington/London: Smithsonian Institution Press, 2001).

14. Kuznick and Gilbert, *Rethinking Cold War Culture*, pp. 10, 11.

15. Douglas Dreishpoon and Alan Trachtenberg, eds. *The Tumultuous Fifties: A View from the New York Times Photo Archives* (New Haven/London: Yale University Press, 2001). The quotations are from Trachtenberg's introduction, "Picturing History in the Morgue," pp. 23, 29, 31.

16. Robert E. Elder, *The Information Machine: The United States Information Agency and American Foreign Policy* (Syracuse, New York: Syracuse University Press, 1968), p. 39. See also Frank Ninkovich, *The Diplomacy of Ideas: U.S. Foreign Policy and Cultural Relations, 1938–1950* (Cambridge: Cambridge University Press, 1981), and Eric J. Sandeen, *Picturing an Exhibition: The Family of Man and 1950s America* (Albuquerque: University of New Mexico Press, 1995).

17. Nicholas Natanson, "Old Frontiers, New Frontiers: Reassessing USIA and State Department Photography of the Cold War Era," paper presented at the Conference on the Power of Free Inquiry and Cold War International History, http://www.archives.gov/research_room_/research_topics/cold_war_history/_conference/natanson.

18. Quoted by Natanson, "Old Frontiers, New Frontiers."

19. Ibid.

20. According to the group caption to a set of slides from Silver Spring,

Maryland. Environmental Protection Agency's DOCUMERICA Project File: 412-DM-136–5–32.

21. There is another interesting piece, relevant in this context, by Nicholas Natanson: "From Sophie's Alley to the White House: Rediscovering the Visions of Pioneering Black Government Photographers," special issue of *Federal Records and African American History* 29, 2 (Summer 1997).

22. As quoted by Max Kozloff, "New York: Capital of Photography," in Kozloff, ed., *New York: Capital of Photography* (New Haven/London: Yale University Press, 2002), p. 55.

23. Edward Steichen, "Introduction," *The Family of Man* (New York: The Museum of Modern Art, 1955), p. 3.

24. Susan Sontag, *Regarding the Pain of Others* (New York: Farrar, Straus and Giroux, 2003).

25. John Steinbeck, *A Russian Journal*, with pictures by Robert Capa (New York: Viking Press, 1948).

26. The quotations are from Lili Corbus Bezner, *Photography and Politics in America: From the New Deal into the Cold War* (Baltimore: Johns Hopkins University Press, 1999), p. 135. On Rockefeller's many connections see, e.g., Eva Cockroft, "Abstract Expressionism: Weapon of the Cold War," in: Francis Fascina, ed., *Pollock and After: The Critical Debate* (New York: Harper and Row, 1985), pp. 125–132; Doss, *Benton, Pollock, and the Politics of Modernism*, and Saunders, *Cultural Cold War*.

27. Bezner, *Photography and Politics*, p. 137.

28. On this, see Sandeen, *Picturing an Exhibition*, p. 44.

29. Ibid.

30. As I have argued more at length in my book *If You've Seen One, You've Seen the Mall: Europeans and American Mass Culture* (Urbana/Chicago: University of Illinois Press, 1996). See also John G. Blair, *Modular America: Cross-Cultural Perspectives on the Emergence of an American Way* (Westport, Connecticut: Greenwood Press, 1988).

31. Vicky Goldberg and Robert Silberman, *American Photography: A Century of Images* (San Francisco: Chronicle Books, 1999), pp. 140–141.

32. Alan Sekula, "The Traffic in Photographs," in *Photography against the Grain: Essays and Photo Works, 1973–1983* (Halifax: Press of Nova Scotia College of Art and Design, 1984), p. 95.

33. Marianne Hirsch, *Family Frames: Photography, Narrative, and Postmemory* (Cambridge, Mass.: Harvard University Press, 1997), p. 69.

34. Ibid.

35. Many of these photographs, documenting the show's immense success abroad, are in the United States Information Agency Collection, National Archives, Washington, D.C.

36. The picture is reproduced in Sandeen, *Picturing an Exhibition*, p. 183.

37. See, e.g., Robert W. Rydell, *All the World's a Fair: Visions of Empire at American International Expositions, 1876–1916* (Chicago: University of Chicago Press, 1984), and John G. Blair, "Buffalo Bill and Sitting Bull: The Wild West as a Media Event," in R. Kroes, ed., *The American West as Seen by Europeans and Americans* (Amsterdam: VU University Press, 1989).

38. Eric Sandeen, "'The Show You See with Your Heart': '*The Family of Man*' on Tour in the Cold War World," in Jean Back and Viktoria Schmidt-Linsenhoff, eds., *The Family of Man, 1955–2001. Humanism and Postmodernism: A Reappraisal of the Photo Exhibition by Edward Steichen* (Marburg: Jonas Verlag, 2004), pp. 101–123.

39. As for the covert, CIA-sponsored forms of cultural diplomacy, see Saunders, *Cultural Cold War.* For the Dutch episode in the world tour of "Family of Man," see Marja L. Roholl, "De fototentoonstelling *Wij mensen—The Family of Man* in het Stedelijk Museum in Amsterdam: Een Amerikaans familiealbum als wapen in de Koude Oorlog" (The Photo Exhibition *Wij Mensen—The Family of Man* in the Stedelijk Museum in Amsterdam: An American Family Album as a Weapon in the Cold War), in E. O. G. Haitsma Mulier, L. H. Maas, and J. Vogel, eds., *Het beeld in de spiegel: Historiografische verkenningen* (The Image in the Mirror: Historiographical Explorations) (Hilversum: Verloren, 2000), pp. 133–153.

40. Viktoria Schmidt-Linsenhoff, "Denied Images: The Family of Man and the Shoa," in Back and Schmidt-Linsenhoff, *The Family of Man,* pp. 80–100. The quotation is from p. 95.

41. Robert H. Haddow, *Pavilions of Plenty: Exhibiting American Culture Abroad in the 1950s* (Washington, D.C./London: Smithsonian Institution Press, 1997), particularly chapter 7. Also Michael Krenn, "'Unfinished Business': Segregation and US Diplomacy at the 1958 World's Fair," *Diplomatic History* 20, 4 (1996): 15.

Chapter 6. An Eye Foreign Eye (pp. 129–142)

1. Lili C. Bezner, *Photography and Politics in America: From the New Deal into the Cold War* (Baltimore/London: Johns Hopkins University Press, 1999).

2. Ibid., p. 139.

3. Ibid., p. 154.

4. Volker R. Berghahn, *America and the Intellectual Cold Wars in Europe* (Princeton and Oxford: Princeton University Press, 2001), pp. 117–118, 124.

5. As Ansel Adams, a good friend of Paul Strand, remembers it in his autobiography: "Because he no longer believed in a healthy future for America, Strand moved to France in 1949. He chose not to live and work under the impending fascism toward which he believed America was headed. Luckily, he es-

caped the witch trials led by Joseph McCarthy that horribly scarred the lives of many American artists." Ansel Adams, *An Autobiography* (Boston/New York/London: Little, Brown, and Company, 1996), p. 97.

6. Anne Tucker, "The Photo League," *Creative Camera* no. 223/224 (July/August 1983): 1013.

7. Anne W. Tucker, Clare Cass, and Stephen Daiter, *This Was the Photo League: Compassion and the Camera from the Depression to the Cold War* (Chicago: Stephen Daiter Gallery, 2001).

8. Max Kozloff, ed., *New York: Capital of Photography* (New Haven/London: Yale University Press, 2002), pp. 9–79.

9. Quoted by Bezner, *Photography and Politics,* p. 123.

10. Ibid., p. 123.

11. Ibid., p. 118.

12. Quoted in ibid., p. 186.

13. Tom Maloney, ed., *U.S. Camera Annual 1958* (New York: U.S. Camera, 1957), p. 89.

14. Walker Evans, "Robert Frank," in Maloney, *U.S. Camera Annual 1958,* p. 90.

15. Bezner, *Photography and Politics,* p. 190.

16. Robert Silberman, "*The Americans* in Europe: Text, Context, Reception," in David E. Nye and Mick Gidley, eds., *American Photographs in Europe* (Amsterdam: VU University Press, 1994), p. 245.

17. Bezner, *Photography and Politics,* p. 114.

18. Ibid., p. 191.

19. Kozloff, *New York,* p. 51.

20. Max Kozloff, "William Klein and the Radioactive Fifties," in Max Kozloff, *The Privileged Eye: Essays on Photography* (Albuquerque: University of New Mexico Press, 1994), p. 45.

Chapter 7. Imaginary Americas in Europe's Public Space (pp. 143–169)

1. Frédéric Brenner, *Diaspora: Homelands in Exile* (London : Bloomsbury, 2003).

2. Irene van der Linde and Nicole Segers, *Het einde van Europa: Ontmoetingen langs de nieuwe oostgrens* [The End of Europe: Encounters along the New Eastern Border] (Rotterdam: Lemniscaat, 2004), p. 388.

3. Edward Atiyah, *The Arabs* (Harmondsworth: Penguin Books, 1955).

4. On the history of this myth, see Jan Willem Schulte Nordholt, *The Myth of the West: America as the Last Empire* (Grand Rapids, Michigan: Eerdmans, 1995).

5. Barbie Zelizer, *Remembering to Forget: Holocaust Memory through the Camera's Eye* (Chicago and London: University of Chicago Press, 1998), p. 227.

6. Anne Applebaum, *Between East and West: Across the Borderlands of Europe* (London, 1995), p. 305.

7. Moray McGowan, "'The Bridge of the Golden Horn': Istanbul, Europe and the 'Fractured Gaze from the West' in Turkish writing in Germany," *Yearbook of European Studies* 15 (2000): 53–69.

8. Quoted in Udo Steinbach, "Die Turkei zwischen Vergangenheit und Gegenwart" (Turkey Between the Past and the Present), *Informationen zur politischen Bildung*, 223 (2. Quartal 1989): 43.

9. McGowan, "'Bridge of the Golden Horn,'" p. 54.

10. This is true more generally, it is my impression, for European films shown in the United States. When in the United States, in places such as Boston, New York, or even a small university town like Bloomington, I found it easier to keep up with recent European films than in my hometown of Amsterdam. Important films reached those places, and ran in many cases for many weeks in the various art theaters in the area.

11. For a survey of these European debates I may refer the reader to my book *If You've Seen One, You've Seen the Mall: Europeans and American Mass Culture* (Urbana/Chicago: University of Illinois Press, 1996). For a survey of French views of American modernity, see my chapter on the subject in my book *Them and Us: Questions of Citizenship in a Globalizing World* (Urbana/Chicago: University of Illinois Press, 2000). See also Philippe Roger, *L'ennemi américain: Généalogie de l'antiaméricanisme en France* (Paris: Editions du Seuil, 2002).

12. See, e.g., Rob Kroes, "America and the European Sense of History," in Kroes, *Them and Us.*

13. Roland Robertson, "Globalisation or Glocalisation?" *Journal of International Communication* 1, 1 (1994).

Chapter 8. Shock and Awe in New York City (pp. 170–181)

1. Hal Buell, *Moments: Pulitzer Prize–winning Photographs, a Visual Chronicle of Our Time* (New York: Black Dog and Leventhal Publishers, 2002), pp. 20–24. On the afterlife of this iconic photograph, see David Nye, "Introduction," in David E. Nye and Mick Gidley, eds., *American Photographs in Europe* (Amsterdam: VU University Press, 1994). Also Ralph Blumenthal, "A Son Pierces the Long Silence of a Flag-Raiser," *New York Times*, May 17, 2000.

2. Magnum Photographers, *New York September 11*, introduction by David Halberstam (New York: Powerhouse Books, 2002).

3. Colin Jacobson, ed., *Underexposed* (New York: Vision On Publishing, 2002).

4. Ibid., p.6.

5. "Witness and Response: Remembering September 11," *Library of Congress Information Bulletin* 61, 9 (September 2002). The cover drawing grippingly

shows the Twin Towers, their elongated shapes filled with individual human faces, while jointly forming the number 11.

6. Buell, *Moments,* pp. 266–274.

7. Ibid., p. 273.

8. "The National Security Strategy of the United States of America" (September 2002), http://www.whitehouse.gov/nsc/nss5.html, PDF: http://www.whitehouse.gov/nsc/nss.pdf.

9. *Granta* 77 (Spring 2002): 47–50.

10. We should never forget, though, particularly when it comes to answering the question of "Why others hate us" (or rather, hate the U.S.), that America's internationalism has been at times, to say the least, ambiguous. Suffice it just to remind ourselves of that other September 11, when Salvador Allende, although democratically elected, was ousted from office and killed with the complicity of the CIA.

Index